TRANSITIONING
IN THE
WORKPLACE

TRANSITIONING
IN THE
WORKPLACE

A Guidebook

DANA PIZZUTI

Jessica Kingsley *Publishers*
London and Philadelphia

First published in 2018
by Jessica Kingsley Publishers
73 Collier Street
London N1 9BE, UK
and
400 Market Street, Suite 400
Philadelphia, PA 19106, USA

www.jkp.com

Library of Congress Cataloging in Publication Data
A CIP catalog record for this book is available from the Library of Congress

British Library Cataloguing in Publication Data
A CIP catalogue record for this book is available from the British Library

ISBN 978 1 78592 802 4
eISBN 978 1 78450 822 7

Printed and bound by CPI Group (UK) Ltd, Croydon, CR0 4YY

To my mom, Lillian Pizzuti,
an inspiration and incredible example of fortitude,
determination, rectitude, and grace.

CONTENTS

ACKNOWLEDGMENTS

First and foremost, I would like to thank my wife and soulmate Stella, without whose unwavering support and belief I am not sure I would be where I am today, and who encouraged me to record my experiences which have given rise to this book.

I would also like to thank my children Nick and Sofia, of whom I'm incredibly proud and thankful for their understanding. My stepchildren Delaney and Hayden have welcomed me into their lives and provide a source of learning and tolerance.

I would also like to acknowledge the following individuals for the various roles they have played in my life and in the creation of this book.

My brother Steve and his wife Stacy, for their efforts to keep my name and pronouns straight.

Paula Blay and Peter Wale, who have been friends for so many years and supportive always.

James Everitt and Tom Wildman, the first friends I came out to as I began my journey.

Sir Ian and Darryl Weller, who have always been welcoming and generous to me and my family.

Ken Eng, who has become a close and chosen family member and has been incredibly encouraging to me in living my truth, holding down the fort with our blended family while Stella attended to me for my long-distance surgeries.

Martine Rothblatt, an icon and an inspiration for me and the LGBTQ+ community. I'm thrilled to count her as a friend.

My literary agent Carol Mann, and my editorial advisor Pam Liflander, who helped me get this book out of me and into the hands of readers. I'm grateful for Andrew James and the team at Jessica Kingsley Publishers who believed in the importance of this topic and my inaugural writing effort.

My friends and advisors in the tribulations of my transition: Tiffany Cook and Morgan Martin, as well as Aejaie Sellers and the girls at Carla's, especially Cynthia Norwood, Ashley Campbell, and Lauren.

My therapist Judy Van Maasdam and the incredibly helpful members of her support group, Alice Miller, Jayna Sheats, Lea Roberts, Charlene Dibner, and Roni Culpeper.

My astute attorney, Rick Levine, for his legal advice on my personal journey and his guidance with the manuscript for this book.

My wonderful internist and personal medical advisor, Dr. Kathy Renschler.

My speech therapist, Maureen O'Connor, who taught me so much about my voice and gender cultural norms.

The Dana dream team: Gita Razavi and Sharon Chu at Medical Aesthetics of Menlo Park, who became my friends when I was very vulnerable; Ivy Ruslin, who taught me so much about makeup and became a friend very early on when I needed it most; the very talented hairstylists, Michelle Baldini and Sevan Caneri, who have been so helpful in establishing my look and encouraged me to experiment and become the new me; my electrologist and advisor, Diana Wagner, with whom I have spent one to two hours per week for over two years; my fantastic fashion consultants, personal shoppers, and executives from Barneys, Nancy Rogers Ray, Paul Graham, Lisel Fay, Shannon Donohue, Richard Canciamilla, Isadora Gallardo, Lisa Perry, and Joan Mackman; the personal shoppers from Nordstrom, especially Mary Ow and Joanie Clark.

Dr. Thomas Satterwhite, who did my first surgeries.

The amazing medical team at New York University (NYU), including Dr. Rachel Bluebond-Langner, Dr. Lee Zhao, Kevin Moore, Dr. Aron Janssen, Dr. Richard Greene, and all of their office staff.

Workplace allies include my administrative assistant at my previous company who was a confidante for over five years and made working there more bearable, as well as David Ralston, Korab Zuka, Phebe Kwon, John Aitken, Mike Wulfsohn, Tobias Peschel, Cara Miller, and Clifford Samuel. My tremendous leadership team at my prior company, including Paul Tomkins, Gwenaelle Pemberton, Mike Sobczyk, Fred O'Callaghan, Naumann Chaudry, Jennifer Stephens, Mai Lai, and Michele Anderson who, along with their teams, carried out their duties admirably and to whom I express great appreciation.

The folks at INvolve and OUTstanding, Suki Sandhu, Alexandra Evreinoff, Ori Chandler, and the Transgender Working Group of Antonia Belcher, Stuart Barette, Leng Montgomery, Nicki Burr, Emma Cusdin, and Pips Bunce. Selene Barry and the others at Out & Equal, including Isabel Porras, Calvin Johnson, and members of the Transgender Guidelines committee Jenna Cook, Andre Wilson, and Deborah Drew.

Interviewees Denise Visconti from Littler; Sharon Papo from the Diversity Center in Santa Cruz; Alex Schultz, Nick White, and Genevieve Grdina from Facebook; Patricia Oliverio-Lauderdale and Keith Epstein from Intel; Cory Valente from Dow Chemical; Dr. Renee McLaughlin from Cigna; and Annie Vincent from Salesforce.

Jenna Rapues and Bob Grant from UCSF; Chris Cowen, Mary Cha Caswell, Joe Hollendoner, and the members of the leadership and Board of Directors of the San Francisco AIDS Foundation; David Munar and Cece Hardracker of Howard Brown Health in Chicago; Mara Keisling and the National Center for Transgender Equality.

Bob Press from NYU, who encouraged me to become an infectious disease doctor and was an inspiration early in my career.

And to all of the allies in the wider LGBTQ+ community, which has always been welcoming and supportive.

A note to the reader

Throughout this book, I have used the shorthand acronym LGBTQ+ to refer to the broadest possible community, including lesbian, gay, bisexual, trans, queer/questioning, and intersex individuals. We are all in this together.

Disclaimer

Every effort has been made to ensure that the information contained in this book is correct, but it should not in any way be substituted for medical advice. Readers should always consult a qualified medical practitioner before adopting any complementary or alternative therapies. Neither the author nor the publisher takes responsibility for any consequences of any decision made as a result of the information contained in this book.

In addition, the legal landscape is constantly evolving and there may be changes over time in employment practices at various companies. This book reflects the information available when we went to press.

INTRODUCTION

Almost one percent of the United States (US) population identifies as transgender. Although this is a small percentage compared to the general population, it reflects an estimated 2.25 million people, many of whom are in the workforce and looking to stay there. Yet corporate America is significantly lacking in real and effective workplace guidelines that ensure transgender employees feel welcome and included. According to a 2011 report entitled *Injustice at Every Turn: A Report of the National Transgender Discrimination Survey*,[1] transgender and gender non-conforming people face staggering rates of harassment, mistreatment, and discrimination at work. The most obvious sign of this discrimination is an extremely high unemployment rate: double that of the general population.

Worse, too few companies have policies in place for helping employees navigate the before-during-and-after experiences of a

---

1   Grant, J.M., Mottet, L.A., Tanis, J., Harrison, J., Herman, J.L., and Keisling, M. (2011) *Injustice at Every Turn: A Report of the National Transgender Discrimination Survey.* Washington: National Center for Transgender Equality and National Gay and Lesbian Task Force, pp.50–70.

gender transition. Some of the most progressive companies may offer assistance for managing internal employee communications or clear health insurance guidelines, while others get the experience totally wrong, creating havoc in the workplace and feelings of hopelessness among the employees.

As a transgender rights advocate, I agree with the majority of experts in the field when they say that a lack of understanding of the transgender experience holds large and small companies back from achieving their financial goals. According to a 2015 Out Now Global LGBT+ 2020 Study, *LGBT Diversity, Show Me The Business Case,*[2] there is a quantifiable benefit for businesses when LGBT+ employees are encouraged to come out to all co-workers within an inclusive environment. These benefits relate directly to employee retention. For instance, in the US alone, 67 percent of LGBT+ employees who ranked themselves as "out to all" in the workplace felt that colleagues treated them with respect and as a productive member of the team, compared to 38 percent who were not out to anyone at work.

Yet the total fraction of LGBT+ employees who are out at work in the US is still less than 40 percent. Worse, the data in the Out Now Global LGBT+2030 Study suggests that 21 percent of LGBT+ employees are still not out to anyone in their office. Fifty-five percent of transgender respondents believed that if they came out as trans at work, it would have a negative effect on prospects for future promotions. This number is further supported in the data where even 60 percent of "out to all" LGBT+ employees in Canada believed that they would have to leave their job in order to be promoted.

My hope is that we can change these statistics to make the workplace a more welcoming environment. I want to make the process of coming out and transitioning, especially in the workplace, as stress-free as possible. Considering the magnitude of the emotions behind it and the overwhelming scope of the changes facing the transitioning employee, I believe there is much employers

---

2   Johnson I. and Cooper, D. (2015) *LGBT Diversity: Show Me The Business Case.* Utrecht: Out Now Global.

can do, and those transitioning need to know that there are lots of options available and systems already in place that work. This book is meant to provide a supportive resource for both employers and employees. Had I had a book like this when I transitioned in 2015, I know that things would have gone a lot differently for me, and for my employer. In fact, I would probably still be working at that firm.

Ever since my transition I have been approached by many transgender individuals who want to know how I managed my transition and made it work as a senior executive in the conservative pharmaceutical industry. I wrote this book primarily for those who are contemplating or embarking on a transition, but also for their managers and human resources (HR) departments, so that everyone can have a better understanding of the physical and emotional issues transitioning employees face and can better support those employees as well as their co-workers. Think of it as a roadmap that offers specific guidance for what to expect inside and outside the workplace, how to anticipate, prepare for, and react to the most common situations, and how to minimize frustration and maximize career progress.

My transition

My story begins back when I was a teenager. I remember reading a newspaper article about a new surgery being performed at Johns Hopkins University. This was in the early 1970s, and the article was about a person who had a male-to-female sex change, and in that moment, I realized that I wished to be that person. Having soft lines, curves, breasts, a vagina—I wondered, what would that be like? Even though I was always attracted to girls, I never stopped wishing that I could be one. Whenever I was home alone, I would sneak into my parents' room and try on my mother's bras and panties, including her realistic breast forms that she had had made following a mastectomy, which simulated the weight and feel of a real breast. This secret behavior continued intermittently throughout my adult life, through my undergraduate and medical schooling, two heterosexual marriages, two children, and a flourishing career.

It wasn't until I reached my late 50s that I realized I could no longer live on the sidelines of my own life. I could no longer just accept that I was a guy, and would have to make the best of it. At that time, I was working at a Fortune 100 pharmaceutical firm as a vice president. Although it might sound trite, I'm good at my job, and at the time I was still enjoying working for that company. By 2015, I had been at there for eight years and had achieved remarkable success. I had grown my department from 120 people to over 400, and my team spanned 30 countries. I was busy setting new industry benchmarks for speed and efficiency, and the company was enjoying enormous success and recognition. What's more, I felt we were really making a difference: the company had just obtained five new drug approvals in the previous two years, including two that would cure Hepatitis C, two new combination treatments for HIV (human immunodeficiency virus), and one for leukemia.

My marriage to my second wife was falling apart. When we agreed to separate, I realized I needed to figure out exactly what was going on with my identity. I had always told myself that if I was ever single again I would pursue the identity situation (maybe). Now was my chance and I seized it.

Without the internet, I don't think I would have been able to make decisions as quickly as I did. I found myself spending hours looking online for help, either through websites for the transgender community or YouTube videos which featured individual stories of transition, as well as more mundane issues such as how to apply cosmetics. Eventually I came across a website called "Carla's: The Social Club," described as, "A discreet, safe and private place for the transgender and cross-dressing community." The headline alone seemed very reassuring and private. It was located not too far from my home and offered makeovers, clothing, and a safe place to meet other trans men and women. I called and made an appointment for a consultation. This was the first time I had opened up about my gender confusion to anyone.

Aejaie Sellers was the proprietor of Carla's, having bought the business from Carla herself several years before. I learned that Aejaie was transgender and had transitioned when she was in her late teenage years. The first thing she asked me was if I had chosen a femme name. I didn't even know what she meant at first; I hadn't ever thought about it!

She asked me a bit about my situation and I mentioned that I mainly cross-dressed when I was alone, but had never spoken to anyone about it. Aejaie told me that my situation was similar to other cross-dressers. She joked and asked me what the difference was between being a cross-dresser and transgender: "about two years!" I didn't realize then that the time interval would be considerably shorter for me.

Aejaie helped me find a therapist, Judy Van Maasdam, one of the pre-eminent psychologists in the area who specialized in transgender issues. Judy changed my life. She told me that it was very common for successful men to have a gender revelation late in life. She also mentioned that it was usually a personal disruption or major life event that prompted men to pursue the quest to solve the gender identity issue, such as an illness, death of a partner, or like me, a looming divorce after 26 years of marriage. As she heard about my identity struggles and asked pointed questions, she summed it up and said, "We've got to get you on hormones!"

I bluntly asked whether at my age, having just turned 59, I was too old to begin the process. Her response was all I needed to hear, "You are never too old." She also told me I needed to live as much of my life as I could as a woman to see if transitioning was right for me. She introduced me to a new doctor who would prescribe the hormones, and after a full physical I was given the prescriptions. I was so excited to go to the pharmacy and pick up my prescriptions. I had still not ventured out in public as a woman, so picked them up as a male. When I got home, I hastily took apart the package and read the directions. I noted that the day was May 31, 2014, and from then on I considered that my—Dana's—birthday. Although I knew from my medical training that the hormonal changes would take years to become fully apparent, I began to notice some breast enlargement within a few months and started wearing a sports bra at the suggestion of Aejaie.

Following Judy's advice, for the next nine months I lived a completely double life. I started three more important transitional activities: acquisition of a wardrobe, removal of body hair, and voice training. During the day I was David, the good employee. At night and at weekends I was Dana. I started hanging out with new friends, and less than six months later I was introduced to Stella, who has since become my wife and my soulmate.

After the first six months, I decided to make three overt physical changes to my appearance. I wasn't yet ready to completely transition at my job and with my family, but I felt these would be the right first steps for my eventual emergence as a woman.

I had lost a lot of weight, going from around 195 to 165 pounds. I stopped drinking wine for Lent and then kept going with it, and the pounds melted away and stayed off. The diet wasn't exactly part of my plan, but it did work out well when I was eventually living in stylish female clothes. The first intentional outward decision was to find a hairstylist who would help me with my eventual look as a woman. I was referred to Michele Baldini by my administrative assistant at work, who knew nothing about my gender identity struggles at that time. Second, I had both ears pierced and wore small silver studs, and third, I started paying more attention to my nails, getting professional manicures and keeping the nails short and well-groomed with clear nail polish—not in any way flamboyant or inappropriate for men, at least in my mind. Subconsciously, I was preparing myself to transition at work.

I had never fully understood the importance of corporate culture with respect to diversity and inclusion, but as I began exploring what my life would look and feel like as a woman, I thought about it a lot and wondered how my work life might change after I transitioned. I consulted an attorney to understand the California employment laws, because these regulations are typically handled on the state level. As I considered my future and began to research how I would begin a workplace transition and where I could get support within the company, I found nothing. It was ironic that I was working for the same drug company that was the premier provider of HIV therapies for the LGBTQ+ community, but it had no official HR approach to addressing LGBTQ+ employees, let alone those who were transitioning. The company didn't even have an LGBTQ+ employee support group, an offering that had become increasingly common in other companies under their "inclusion and diversity" programs.

So imagine my surprise when one February day, less than a year after I started seriously but secretly following the path to transition, the HR business partner unexpectedly strolled into my office. She seemed a bit uncomfortable but said she had something to tell me. "Dave, there has been a lot of talk recently about your change in appearance," she began.

"Really?" I responded. "In what respect?"

"Well, your ears are pierced and you are wearing nail polish. There is a feeling among senior management that your appearance is not consistent with the required decorum for a vice president in your position."

My jaw dropped and immediately my mind began racing. Who in senior management feels this way? Who asked you to talk to me? Was my career already irrevocably impacted? Even though I was seriously thinking about transitioning, I just wasn't prepared to make my announcement that particular day.

I slowly gathered my thoughts, and asked, "So what are you telling me? That I should take out the earrings and remove the nail polish?"

"Yes, that would be helpful," the HR lady replied.

"Is my career in jeopardy? Have they determined that I am already on the way out?" I asked.

"I don't think so," she responded. "But if you feel strongly that you need to keep the earrings and the polish to maintain your authenticity, you might want to consider whether this is the right place for you."

My eyes widened. Her response was essentially an ultimatum to change the way I looked in order for me to keep my job. I worried that if I was fired for not complying, as a trans person, I might not ever get a corporate job again at the senior level I currently enjoyed, and everything I accomplished there, and my own growth and reputation as an executive would be gone in an instant. And if I declared right then that I was transgender, would they fire me anyway? Would my colleagues support me, and would my own employees continue to respect me? And if I just meekly did what she asked and went way back into the closet, what would that say about my need to live authentically? I felt completely vulnerable, so I enquired, "Is what you are asking actually discrimination against me for my appearance?"

"It's not discrimination, Dave, because you are not a member of a protected class," she replied. Once she walked away, I realized I was much closer to announcing my transition plans than I intended, effectively beginning my journey of transitioning at work. That day was the most emotional, challenging, and frightening day of my life.

I called my attorney and confirmed that the HR encounter could be categorized as workplace discrimination based on gender expression. I didn't fully understand the importance of that fact until my attorney pointed out how blatantly inappropriate HR's behavior was toward me. We decided I would draft an email in which I would state my situation and intentions and I would send it to the HR person and my boss. Then I would go and tell my boss personally.

Although I was supposed to go to an electrolysis session at lunch, I canceled it and continued to mull over the options. I decided I would take out the earrings (which I really didn't want to do since the holes might close up), but figured I needed to get through the day without inviting any more criticism. I also went to the nail salon and had the clear polish removed. However, no matter how many ways I looked at it, my decision was the same: I needed to be true to myself, and even though I didn't think I was ready to declare myself that day, my options were limited. The scariest aspect was that once I started, I could not take back this decision. I needed to be ready to accept the consequences, even if I was not completely sure whether it would turn out well or not.

Just before I went to meet with my boss, I sent an email to HR stating that I was transgender, I had made the decision to transition at work, I had no intention to leave the company, my colleagues would be able to understand and support my change, and I could accomplish my transition in a professional manner consistent with workplace norms. (You can read the full email in Chapter 4.) Nothing was the same after that. Within a few months, I successfully began my workplace transition. I stayed there for another two years before I was recruited to Rigel Pharmaceuticals. I am in a very similar position there: Senior Vice President of Regulatory Affairs and Clinical Compliance, and I love my job. More importantly, I feel completely accepted at work for who I am.

I've since made a complete medical and surgical transition and have become an outspoken advocate for transgender rights. I participated as a senior executive in the Out & Equal Executive Forum in San Francisco and led a Transgender Leadership panel for them at their annual summit. I have participated in panel discussions on access to healthcare at the Howard Brown Midwest LGBTQ Healthcare summit in Chicago and have been asked to join the Trans Awareness Working Group, sponsored by OUTstanding, an LGBTQ+ business executive networking group based in the UK. I was also elected to the Board of Directors of the San Francisco AIDS Foundation as its only trans board member.

Today, I'm happier and more at peace than I ever could imagine. And I want everyone who is contemplating or embarking on a transition to know that there are resources and support available every step of the way. First and foremost, being gender non-conforming is not an illness or a mental deficiency—it is a characteristic, like personality type. Our ability to accept and address this attribute is within our control and is the beginning of a process of self-discovery and fulfillment that can be satisfying and especially rewarding.

The decision to transition is one of the most daunting and complicated turning points in life. Personal and psychological questions, family realities including spouses, children, and parents, medical and surgical decisions, and the legal and employment ramifications are arduous issues that can take years or decades to navigate. Making the decision and beginning to transition takes real courage—the kind of courage that has proved to be an asset in the workplace. A transitioning employee experiences intense emotional challenges, new fears, and hurdles every day, but is almost universally respected for having the fortitude to accept the consequences of being openly authentic. In fact, making this committment exemplifies many prized attributes exceptional employees have: the ability to search for causes of a problem (such as gender dysphoria), the willingness to consider various alternatives to resolve an issue (such as cataloging the potential implications of a transition), and the willingness to make a reasoned decision, move forward and accept the consequences. The character and fortitude displayed by anyone who decides to transition should be a reason not only to support but to seek out transgender employees as clear-eyed, hard-working, analytical, and decisive people.

Setting best practices

My goal for this book is to establish a set of best practices so that anyone, with any type of job, can successfully transition to their most authentic self. I promise to be completely candid about every aspect of my transition, and reveal in stark detail what to expect, and how to anticipate, prepare, and react to specific situations at work, ranging from notifying HR to telling your boss, and how to minimize frustration and maximize career progress.

Along the way, I will explore all facets of a successful transition in the workplace from a myriad of perspectives, including:

- performing a comprehensive assessment of gender identity and expression, including readiness to transition

- preparing for family complications

- establishing a realistic medical timeline for therapies and surgeries, as well as taking a comprehensive look at the choices and procedures currently available

- understanding anti-discrimination laws and protections for trans people on both the federal and state levels

- managing and cultivating interpersonal relationships between subordinates, peers, and management

- identifying and establishing a support system at work

- dealing with difficult colleagues and customers

- finding effective ways to job search: how to address resumes and credentials after a transition

- establishing a comprehensive list of the best places for trans people to work in the US.

Let's get started

There is no way for me to know where you currently are on the path to a complete transition, so let's start at the beginning. In the next chapter, you'll begin the self-investigative work to decide if you are ready to transition in any setting: at home or at work. In my case, making the decision to transition finally relieved all my internal doubts, and I feel privileged to have been able to become who I really am and to provide support for others facing this choice.

PART I

PREPARING TO TRANSITION

CHAPTER 1

CONDUCTING A PERSONAL SITUATION ANALYSIS

Anyone contemplating a transition faces a multitude of decisions. Each decision builds on the previous one, creating a path forward to a new life both in and out of work. In order to start making these decisions, I believe you need to connect with a grounded idea of where you are emotionally and physically, what you may be afraid of, and who is there to support you.

Psychiatrist Aron Janssen has been seeing transgender patients exclusively since 2011 at the Gender and Sexuality Service at New York University (NYU) Langone Health. Dr. Janssen told me that he typically sees a few general categories of individuals who are in distinct places along their journey. The first group includes people who are just addressing their thoughts and feelings about their gender identity. The second are people who have already made the decision to transition but need a psychiatrist's help accessing the appropriate medical interventions. The third group falls somewhere in between: they want to transition and need help figuring out how best to do it, including navigating the "coming out" to friends, family, partners/spouses, and work.

Dr. Janssen believes, as I do, that allowing yourself the opportunity and the time to be introspective, thorough, information-seeking, and thoughtful about the transition will set you up for the most positive experience. If you have been wanting to transition for a long time and are focused on the goal, you can be so blinded by your sense of urgency that you dismiss both logical steps as well as potential setbacks. It is human nature to expect the best, but I believe that the unknown is what really makes people feel afraid. The more you know what to expect, both good and bad, the more prepared you are for every aspect of the transition, and the better off you will be.

Slowing the process down and making sure you are emotionally and physically ready is the goal for this chapter. Transitioning has substantial emotional challenges and knowing them up front and creating a game plan for how you will deal with them is key. There is a dizzying array of issues you are going to be dealing with, so let's start at the very beginning. The first step is to assess exactly where you are in terms of gender dysphoria, how you are presenting to the rest of the world and who you can count on for support throughout the transition. I strongly feel that the first person you have to get on your team is a qualified and empathetic therapist who is a good fit for your needs and personality.

Work with a therapist

Working with a therapist is critical for beginning a medical transition. I always knew that there was something different about me. I always had secret desires to be female, but I was so closeted that I never reached out to talk to a professional therapist about my gender concerns until later in life. But after so many years of having this secret desire, there came a point where I realized that I needed to talk to somebody about it. Once I started going to therapy, I wished I had gone earlier.

A good therapist will be your confidential and experienced ally, especially if you aren't ready to tell anyone. When I first started seeing my therapist, Judy Van Maasdam, I wasn't ready to tell anyone else. My fear surrounding the repercussions of my kids and co-workers learning my secret completely overshadowed my need to tell anybody. However, Judy was so supportive that she allayed my fears; otherwise, I'm not sure I would have ever been ready to transition.

Many transgender folks have told me that they were so worried about saying something that will prevent the therapist from endorsing future medical treatment (specifically hormones). I have spoken with many healthcare providers, including therapists, internists, and surgeons, and they uniformly state that this worry is completely unfounded: there is no "right" or "wrong" answer to any question. A good therapist will understand what you are going through, so just be honest and they will help you.

Finding a good therapist may not be difficult at all but finding the right therapist for you may take some time. Most importantly, you want to connect with someone who has a practice that focuses on gender dysphoria or transgender patients. These therapists have an empathetic and thorough understanding of what concerns you and will know exactly how they can help you. The best option is to find a therapist and meet with them in person. If you live in a remote area, you might not have many options for in-person therapy. But even in small towns, we are starting to find doctors and therapists who are educated and exposed to the trans community.

Excellent resources for finding transgender support include:

- World Professional Association for Transgender Health (WPATH): the website has a dropdown menu to locate practitioners for various specialties who are members of this premier organization (www.wpath.org).

- American Psychiatric Association: provides useful information about gender dysphoria, support groups, and finding a psychiatrist (www.psychiatry.org).

- LGBT CenterLink: this is a way to find an LGBTQ+ support center anywhere in the US. These centers often provide the names for support groups and local health/mental health providers for transgender care (www.LGBTcenters.org).

- TransHealthCare Surgeon Directory: a worldwide directory built on the largest and most comprehensive database of surgeons performing gender reassignment surgery and related procedures. They will be able to refer to other local providers for mental health services (www.transhealthcare.org).

- University medical centers and community health centers: many have renowned transgender programs, such as the University of California—San Francisco, NYU Langone Health, Mount Sinai Medical Center, and Callen-Lorde Community Health Center in New York City, Fenway Health in Boston, and Howard Brown Health in Chicago. More of these centers are opening every year, so check with your local hospital or university.

- National Alliance on Mental Illness (NAMI): a national network of mental healthcare providers, as well as a provider database (www.nami.org/Find-Support/LGBTQ).

- National Council for Behavioral Health: national network of community behavioral health centers, as well as a provider database (www.thenationalcouncil.org).

- Psychology Today Therapist Finder: a list of therapists around North America. Once a city or state is selected, there is a filter for therapists working with transgender clients under the 'Issue' area on the left-hand menu (https://therapists. psychologytoday.com/rms).

Many sites can even arrange for telephone consultations, which are critical for those who live outside major metropolitan areas. If you are fortunate to live near a large city, you may find that you have many options to choose from. I've also found that if you're around a large university with a medical center or a graduate school that teaches counseling, you can find some very good resources.

Once you find the right therapist, you'll be able to set the parameters of a successful therapeutic relationship. A therapist should be able to tell you up front how many times they typically meet with a client. The answer might vary, depending on the number of topics or concerns you want to discuss. You may even find that having a non-threatening, completely impartial person to support you is something you'll want to continue for a very long time. Ultimately, the most important thing to remember is that the therapeutic relationship is confidential and completely guided by you.

There are pros and cons to using a therapist a friend has recommended. If you know someone who has gone through a similar experience and they had a great therapist, you can be confident that they will be able to address your concerns. But the reality is that finding a great therapist is like finding a soulmate. It's a very personal relationship, so what might have worked for a friend might not work for you.

Unfortunately, and in rare instances, a therapist can do more harm than good. Some are just not supportive or helpful. There is no specific training or certification required to qualify as an "expert" in transgender care. In order to find a good therapist, you have to be a smart patient. Some red flags that will show a lack of empathy or understanding for your particular needs include:

- the use any type of slang (derogatory or otherwise)

- an insensitivity or reluctance to using your preferred pronouns

- the use of the term "transgendered" (with an -ed on the end) or "transsexual"

- a lack of basic knowledge relating to the larger community; for example, if they don't know what the Q stands for in LGBTQ+ or are not familiar with the terms non-binary or gender non-conforming.

According to the WPATH guidelines, the training of mental health professionals considered competent to work with gender dysphoric adults can include any discipline that prepares mental health professionals for clinical practice, such as psychology, psychiatry, social work, mental health counseling, marriage and family therapy, nursing, or family medicine with specific training in behavioral health and counseling. The following are recommended minimum criteria for mental health professionals who work with adults presenting with gender dysphoria:

- A master's degree or its equivalent in an accredited clinical behavioral science field. The mental health professional should have documented credentials from a relevant licensing board.

- Competence in using the *Diagnostic Statistical Manual of Mental Disorders* and/or the *International Classification of Diseases* for diagnostic purposes.

- Ability to recognize and diagnose co-existing mental health concerns and to distinguish these from gender dysphoria.

- Documented supervised training and competence in psycho-therapy or counseling.

- Knowledge of gender non-conforming identities and expressions, and the assessment and treatment of gender dysphoria.

- Continuing education in the assessment and treatment of gender dysphoria. This may include attending relevant professional meetings, workshops, or seminars; obtaining supervision from a mental health professional with relevant experience; or participating in research related to gender non-conformity and gender dysphoria.

In addition to these minimum criteria, it is recommended that mental health professionals are knowledgeable about current community, advocacy, and public policy issues relevant to transgender clients and their families.

Assessing your gender questions

Gender is traditionally considered as binary, either male or female. In some cases, it might be both, which is referred to as *gender fluid* for those who express themselves as male or female depending on their preference at the time, or neither, which is referred to as *non-binary* for those who do not consider themselves on the binary spectrum at all.

Many people think of gender as existing on this binary spectrum: male or female, or somewhere in between. Along this spectrum, we have our original gender assignment, and there is also one's gender identity, gender expression, and sexual orientation or attraction. Gender identity is how you define your preferred gender choice. Gender expression is the way you present yourself through your dress, your actions, and your demeanor. Your sexual orientation or attraction, which is who you are romantically or sexually attracted to, is also a completely separate consideration from the others. There are many possible combinations of these characteristics. A helpful website which can convey these concepts is called the Genderbread Person and can be found at www.genderbread.org.

A therapist's role is to help you find answers to your questions surrounding your gender identity. They can help educate you regarding the diversity of gender identities and expressions and the various options available to alleviate gender dysphoria. They can assist you as you explore various options, with the goals of finding a comfortable gender role and expression, and becoming prepared to make a fully informed decision about available medical interventions, if needed.

All good therapists will begin the conversation by talking to you about *gender dysphoria*. According to the American Psychiatric Association, gender dysphoria is defined as discomfort or distress caused by:

a conflict between a person's physical or assigned gender and the gender with which he/she/they identify. People with gender dysphoria may be very uncomfortable with the gender they were assigned, sometimes described as being uncomfortable with their body (particularly developments during puberty) or being uncomfortable with the expected roles of their assigned gender.[1]

Gender dysphoria is not the same as *gender non-conformity*, which, according to the Institute of Medicine, refers to the extent to which a person's gender identity, role, or expression differs from the cultural norms prescribed for people of a particular sex. Examples of gender non-conformity (also referred to as gender expansiveness or gender fluidity) include girls behaving and dressing in ways more socially expected of boys, or occasional cross-dressing in adult men. Only some gender non-conforming people experience gender dysphoria at some point in their lives. Gender dysphoria and gender non-conformity are also not the same as being gay or lesbian.

Even if you haven't told anyone about your desire to transition, and you're cross-dressing on your own privately, quantifying how much dysphoria you feel is a good place to start. The amount of distress caused by gender dysphoria and gender non-conformity is the issue a therapist wants to address and treat, not the fact that you experience it. Having a gender dysphoria diagnosis is what facilitates access to healthcare and guides your treatment options. The fact that you are "gender non-conforming" is not an illness or a mental health concern; it is a characteristic, like your personality. Therapists who specialize in gender understand this fact and their major concern will always be how your gender dysphoria affects your daily life, and how it should be treated. The point of these statements is to reassure you: there is no blame, and there is nothing "wrong" with you.

---

1   www.psychiatry.org/patients-families/gender-dysphoria/what-is-gender-dysphoria.

However, it would not be realistic to believe that there is no stigma, prejudice, or discrimination against people who transition. Psychologists refer to living with this social stigma, or any other minority position as *minority stress*. Living with this stress can make transgender or gender non-conforming individuals more vulnerable to developing mental health concerns, such as anxiety and depression. A stigma can also contribute to abuse and neglect in one's relationships with peers and family members, which in turn can lead to psychological distress.

ARE YOU GENDER FLUID OR NON-BINARY?

These are emerging concepts within the gender non-conforming community and are becoming more recognized and accepted, particularly within popular culture. Gender fluid refers to the desire to go back and forth to any point on the binary spectrum: sometimes male, sometimes female. Non-binary means that you do not have a desire to identify as either male or female. For non-binary individuals, the correct pronoun use would be "they," "them," and "theirs." These pronouns are continually evolving: recently the use of "ze" or "zir" have been used to refer to individuals whose gender is not known or when a person is neither male nor female in gender.

Questions therapists want you to ponder

Have you told anyone about your gender questions and desires? If you have confided to anyone and had a positive or supportive response, these people can be an emotional resource or an ally as you contemplate your transition. These are people you already trust. For instance, there was a time before I transitioned at work where I was living in two separate worlds and I didn't let them intersect. By day I was Dave, and at night and at weekends I was Dana. However, once I told someone who had known me as Dave that I knew I was trans, I was creating an intersection of both worlds, which for me was at first both scary and risky.

One of the most anxious times of my life was when I was first telling someone from my old life my intentions for a new one. For instance, after I separated from my wife of 26 years, there was a time when I was dressing and living differently at work from how I was on the weekends. I was living as Dave at work and with my two children, and as Dana among my new friends. At some point, with the help of my therapist and a support group she ran, I realized I just couldn't continue living this way, and started to develop a plan to fully transition so that I could live as my most authentic self with all of my various relationships. The first people I told about my plans were James and Tom, a couple I met at my children's school, who I continued to stay friendly with after my wife and I divorced. They had invited me over for dinner at their house one evening, and I decided that I could trust them. I walked them through my recent gender odyssey. As I hoped, they were amazingly supportive. Before I left their home that night James had already changed my contact information to Dana in his phone!

Their positive response made me more comfortable, but my personal goal was to keep this information private until I was ready to transition at work. I had two issues to deal with: my office and my children. I also believe that withholding your intention to transition from others has an additional advantage in that it gives you a little more flexibility and at the same time, control about when and how you come out.

Are you sure you are ready to transition? This question may be the toughest to answer. However, in order to move forward, you need to honestly assess your conviction of your gender identity, and your commitment to living authentically in all relationship contexts. For me, I knew that I was ready to transition when I was actually feeling comfortable as Dana and could contrast those feelings with how I felt as my old self. Once I found that I was looking for more opportunities to be Dana rather than Dave, I realized that I had to transition completely in all aspects of my life.

My friend Morgan had a similar experience. Growing up as a girl in a very conservative, small community in rural Wyoming, Morgan always felt that something wasn't aligning, but didn't address his gender dysphoria until he was 18. When he was about three years old, he was sitting around the dinner table with his parents and his brothers and asked, "When am I going to get my penis?" At college at Montana State University, he enrolled in a human sexuality class and for the first time realized that there were other people who shared similar gender identity feelings. Morgan did not self-identify as trans until the age of 27, when he decided to transition. His family was immediately supportive and no one was surprised by the news, yet there were still several questions about what the transition would entail.

If you don't think you are ready to transition right now, that's okay. It's perfectly reasonable to have concerns or hesitations. There are many people who don't want to transition at all and enjoy their gender fluidity, or don't want to be permanently labeled as either sex. Wherever you are on the spectrum, keep reading. There is plenty you can learn from this book that might make your work life easier now, and going forward, if and when you make a final decision.

If you are ready, start thinking about how you want to handle both the social and medical aspects of transitioning. I've met a few people who have physically transitioned yet are still not completely socially transitioned, either at work or at home. For instance, some male-to-female individuals I've met still attempt and expect to exert their male privilege in the workplace. Some are not mentally or socially prepared for the rejection that can sometimes come with transition, or the personal difficulties women in general face, especially in the workplace.

I've learned that the same aspects of interpersonal relationships I've struggled with pre-transition still exist post-transition. For instance, the dating issue can be challenging both before and after the transition. I knew I was still attracted to women but wasn't sure whether I considered myself to be a lesbian, or whether a lesbian would want a transgender woman as a partner. Fortunately, I met Stella, my current wife, when I was presenting as Dana, even though I had not yet even come out to my children or transitioned at work. It was very affirming that I found someone who was attracted to the real me.

Assessing family relationships

It's very common that trans people will be out to a different extent in different relationships, leaving them in a situation of navigating varying degrees of their transition simultaneously. Dr. Aron Janssen told me that one of the challenges he frequently sees is that even though many of his patients have been grappling with the decision to transition for a long time, when they finally reach the point that they're ready to transition, they become frustrated when the folks surrounding them need time to adjust.

It's important to expect that the process of transition requires a period of adjustment, not only for you, but for everyone else. When you transition, so does the rest of your family. Just remember that their initial reactions are not necessarily predictive of their long-term support. To my mind and in discussions with other transgender individuals, the most significant fear layered within familial relationships is that of rejection. It is quite likely that you will experience some degree of rejection from your immediate and extended family, due not only to the complicated nature of gender identity, but also to the different types of family relationships, family morals, culture, and geography.

If you are currently married or in a relationship, your primary family member is your spouse or partner. Ask yourself the following questions before you broach the topic with them:

- Is your partner aware of you cross-dressing or has he or she participated in role play with you?

- Has your partner accepted or encouraged your consideration of a transition?

- If your partner is not aware of your gender identity questions or desire to transition, do you have an otherwise strong relationship?

- If your partner is not aware, do you think he or she is open-minded enough to understand your transgender identity questions?

If the answer to any of these questions is yes, there may be a willingness on the part of the partner to accept your transition, and in fact, support and encourage you. However, if the answers to these questions are equivocal or negative, then you need to do a different kind of planning. You need to think about, unfortunately, what would happen if that relationship ended.

There is no hard and fast rule for how to discuss a transition within the family. I was more comfortable introducing the topic as my old self (Dave) and then stating that I had been doing some self-assessment and realized I was transgender, and that I intended to transition. I don't believe that it's a great idea to just appear one day as your new self and expect others to understand what is happening. I think it's important to lay the foundation with a discussion about how one feels inside, so that the visual of a change in outward appearance is easier to process.

I've seen and heard about many different outcomes that have been dependent on a particular situation, what a partner is like, what kind of family they came from, and how open-minded they are. Probably the most important factor is the current strength of your relationship. My marriage was breaking up when I decided to transition, and we were already separated. I knew that my ex-wife was not open-minded enough to have me broach the subject with her: she is very traditional, especially when it comes to gender roles. I do sometimes regret that I didn't share my inner questions about my gender identity with her earlier and give her the chance to either help me with it or end the marriage. However, I can't say that I really knew or accepted that I was trans until after the marriage ended. In any case, my understanding of my ex-wife at the time led me to believe she would not have stayed in the marriage. And, the course of action she might have taken in a state of anger or retaliation might have destroyed any chance of having a successful transition at work. I couldn't take the chance: I had too much at stake with my career and my desire to stay in my job.

There are many examples of those who have been in stable relationships and their partner has been extremely supportive and they have stayed together. Morgan as a woman was in a relationship with Tiffany, who was always very much aware that Morgan wanted to transition and supported it. It was almost understood in their relationship that they could be whoever they wanted to be.

There are other situations where the partner was at first not as accepting of the transition. For example, Antonia Belcher decided to transition after leading a double life for five years. When she was fully prepared to transition, she told me, "I couldn't continue to cheat and lie to all the people that were important to me. I found it very hard to like myself when I knew I was lying to all the people that mattered, my wife, my kids, my parents." When she first approached her wife, she said, "I'm going to tell you something now that's going to change everything. It's going to change your world, change your life. Once I've told you, you should divorce me. You should clean me out for as much as you can. Find a new man and restart your life. I'm sorry, but I just know I need to tell you this."

Antonia's wife struggled immensely for a two-year period. But Antonia told me, "She never threw me out and she never asked me to leave. She wanted me to be Antonia on my own time and not let it affect the family. I complied for a while, but I needed to give Antonia a full life, a genuine life." Antonia gave her wife the space she needed, and today, two years later, they remain married. Even though Antonia's wife needed time to adjust, she eventually came around and decided that life was still going to be better with her partner as Antonia, her preferred self, as opposed to the person that she married.

It's hard to predict in any individual situation what's going to happen after the initial disclosure. But it's important to realize that despite the best intentions and being honest with people, the outcome will often depend on the willingness of the spouse or partner to accept a new situation.

Remember, for every ending, there's a beginning. In my case, even though my marriage had already ended, I knew myself well enough that I always believed I would find the right relationship with another person who would love and accept me. Even before my medical transition I met Stella, who is now my wife and soulmate. There is somebody for everyone.

TRUSTING YOUR SPOUSE OR PARTNER

If you are still in the assessment stage and can't trust that your spouse will be supportive, then you may need to keep your disclosure private until you are completely clear about what your path is going to be. One unsupportive or vengeful spouse or partner can cause significant damage by telling your children or your friends or your boss before you are ready. Before you can do damage control you might very quickly be widely outed, especially in this age of social media. You need to consider the potential fallout. Start thinking about how you would like to handle the conversation with your children, how you could prepare yourself emotionally, financially, and legally for a divorce, and how you will navigate the transition by yourself. I've seen situations where as soon as one partner discloses, the other files for divorce and separates, and if there are children, can try to take the children away. This is where your therapist will be a very useful resource.

Telling your children

The second most important familial relationship is that with your children, whose experiences with your transition will vary greatly depending on their ages and whether they are already aware of your gender identity questions. If you have a supportive spouse, it doesn't matter how old your children are—the conversation and your continued relationship with them can go well.

If your spouse or partner is not supportive, all sorts of other complications can arise. The spouse may either take the children away or refuse to allow you to transition in front of them. Or, the spouse may want to be part of the disclosure.

Ideally, your children should first learn about your plans to transition directly from you, predicated on the state of the relationship and the age and maturity of the children. These conversations need to be tailored to your particular situation, but the most important thing is to be honest. I don't think you should just show up cross-dressed in front of your kids without talking to them. Have the conversation as your "old self."

To any child you can say, "I've been doing a lot of soul searching and I went to talk to somebody. I realized I'm transgender. There are things about me that are going to change, like the way I look and dress. And there are going to be things about me that aren't going to change, like the way I love you. I love you and will always love you, but I need to do this for me. From now on we're going have to deal with my transition as a family."

Be calm, answer their questions, leave the conversation open for discussion. In reality, these are just basic good parenting techniques for dealing with any kind of change. For the littlest children, finding a picture book might be helpful. The youngest children may actually be very open-minded. And as long as they don't get a lot of negativity from your spouse or external sources, they can generally go with the flow pretty easily.

Teenagers are typically starting to exert their independence. Depending how strong your relationships are with them, there may be more openness. According to Jean M. Twenge, a psychologist who teaches at San Diego State University and is author of *iGen: Why Today's Super-Connected Kids Are Growing Up Less Rebellious, More Tolerant, Less Happy—and Completely Unprepared for Adulthood—and What That Means for the Rest of Us*,[2] today's teens are very interested in fairness and equality, and are less concerned about gender stereotypes. They are more likely to be exposed through popular media to a wide variety of lifestyles. They may even be struggling with their own gender non-conforming issues. They also may be very worried about what their friends would think about you being trans.

Unfortunately, the most concerning aspect of the situation is what might happen to your children outside the home—they may be bullied or ridiculed. The thing you need to worry about more is their peers at school and how you're going to inoculate them against negative external influences. Whether this happens may depend greatly on where you live and how open and progressive their school and friends are. I think it is paramount to tell your kids how much you love them and that you will always be their parent, even if you look different.

Therapists can be very useful preparing you for and even helping you have these conversations with your children. You can talk to therapists and go to family counseling. Therapists are usually willing to speak with your children to help explain to them and answer their questions. They're not going to give all the details, but they will talk to your children about what you're going through. For example, my therapist offered to talk to my kids. My kids never took her up on it, but the offer was there.

---

2   Twenge, J.M. (2017) *iGen: Why Today's Super-Connected Kids Are Growing Up Less Rebellious, More Tolerant, Less Happy—and Completely Unprepared for Adulthood—and What That Means for the Rest of Us.* New York, NY: Atria Books.

When I told my children, my daughter Sofia was 17 and still living with my ex-wife, and my son Nick was 21 and away at college. They were the first family members I told about my plans besides my ex-wife. I learned a lot from their reactions about the best ways to talk to others about my transition.

I was spending the day with my daughter and we ended up at a restaurant. I made the decision that I wanted to tell her about my plans, but I wasn't sure what would be the best time or the right environment. I ended up telling her while we were out to dinner, but in retrospect, the news would have been received better if I had chosen a more private setting. Because I was so tentative, I realize now that I was not as complete as possible in delivering the details of my plan. I also asked her to keep our conversation a secret, which in retrospect didn't serve either one of us well. When she eventually spoke to my ex-wife about my plans, Sofia realized that I had not been as forthright as I had been with her mother, and she was understandably upset with me. Consequently, my daughter and I didn't talk much for the next several months while she was in high school and living with her mother. In truth, the way she dealt with me was influenced by the fact that many aspects of her personal life were precarious: she was coming to grips with the college admissions process, the divorce, and the fact that her mom would be selling the family house and moving back to the East Coast. Yet today, three years later, my daughter and I have a great relationship. What she realizes is that I can be the same good parent even though I'm a different gender from what I was before. From my point of view, my parenting of her and the advice I give her hasn't changed. I would have made the same parenting decisions as a guy in terms of advice around growing up, as well as her career decisions. But I did learn that honesty, even with your children, is crucial for explaining such a big change in one's life. In retrospect, I should have shared my transition very differently with my daughter: in a private setting and with a more complete disclosure.

The conversation with my son was much smoother because I had learned from my mistakes. I talked to Nick privately when we were taking a walk, and he had an easier time accepting my transition because he was in college, and he had experience with gender non-conforming classmates. He was happy for me, and we have been able to maintain as good a relationship as we ever had.

I strongly believe that the ability to be true to who you are makes you a better parent, because you're more at ease with yourself. I definitely felt guilty keeping this secret from my children. Even though my ex-wife didn't want me to tell them because she thought they couldn't handle it, I felt it was better to be honest and take the consequences, which were very painful for a short period of time with my daughter.

Your parents and siblings

The third level of familial relationships includes parents and siblings, who might have very different reactions from what you might expect, especially if there was unspoken knowledge of your gender issues. Addressing extended family members can pose its own set of challenges, depending on the closeness of the family and its social and religious customs.

When I decided to transition, my parents had already passed away. When I told my brother, we met in person, and he was actually upset because I hadn't told him sooner. He had a friend who transitioned from male to female, so he was pretty familiar with what I would be going through. Initially he was shocked, but when he thought about it he realized that on some level he was aware of the struggles I had growing up. Now, he is very supportive. He tries to call me Dana, and when he makes a mistake, I can see he feels bad about it.

Overall, I've found that just as in all aspects of life, no two people are the same, and no two reactions may be the same. Some will need more time than others. My son and brother were the quickest to accept, while my daughter and my ex-wife needed more time. I've also heard stories of parents taking years to come to terms with the transition of an adult child. Be patient; give the important people in your life the time and space they need to process this change. If you are important to them, you can be hopeful that they will eventually accept you for who you are. And when someone doesn't, you will know that you did your best to explain why you had to live your truth.

Workplace relationships

The relationships you have with others in the workplace are crucial to the success of your transition at work. The nature and culture of the business, how employees work together and report to the different lines of authority, as well as the company's geographic location may also be important factors to consider.

Your workplace comprises different categories of people. There are co-workers, supervisors, senior management, and, for some, subordinates and customers. Your particular experience will be dependent on the proportions you have of each of those groups, and where you stand on the corporate ladder.

You will also have different types of relationships with each of these groups of people. Some work relationships become personal friendships, and one important variable is how much intersectionality you have with your office and your personal life. If you have a spouse or partner who is not particularly supportive and could out you publicly to your social circle, it might affect your relationships at work very quickly.

In my case, the chief operating officer at my company had a daughter who went to school with my daughter. My daughter was afraid that if I came out at work, it would get around at school and affect her school life. That particular worry didn't materialize, but this type of issue can cross over into multiple parts of your life.

The following questions about your current workplace relationships will help you evaluate how successful your transition at work could be, and if you are at a place where you will be happy to stay working after your transition.

- Is the culture of the office more progressive or conservative?

- Are you in an industry like academia, technology, or media, which are inherently more progressive; or science, finance, or sales, which are more conservative?

- Does your company have a diversity and inclusion group, which is usually part of the HR department?

- Does your company have harassment and discrimination guidelines and training?

- Is there an LGBTQ+ employee group?

- What are the demographics of senior management and co-workers?

- Are there any "out" LGBTQ+ top executives or members of senior management?

- Do you think your co-workers, from the boss to your peers to your subordinates, will continue to respect you, and will you all be able to continue to work well together?

In today's political and financial climate, some people report that they would rather not transition, depending on how much they want to keep their job or whether they feel more likely to experience discrimination, and they feel that it will be difficult for them to achieve their ideal gender identity. They don't want to take a chance. However, if they understood how their colleagues would actually react, if they might be open-minded and supportive, they may come to a healthier, more proactive decision.

In many cases, your co-workers will actually be open-minded and may laud you as a transgender person for being brave or courageous. According to an HR expert who came to see me when I was planning my notification at work, and who specializes in supporting transgender transitions in the workplace, transitions very often go quite well, and the greatest source of concern is the anxiety of the soon to be transitioning employee. Your co-workers may experience their own worry about referring to you by the wrong name or pronoun, and thereby offending you.

Just like family, your co-workers may need time to process your transition. Their reactions will also be influenced by their own history and their own views about gender. Remember, these views can fluctuate as people become more acclimatized, and some will come around to any sort of change sooner than others.

Enlisting support

It is very important to enlist support as you contemplate or embark on your transition, especially from those outside the workplace who can help you navigate the process. These individuals might be able to provide moral support and advice, and help you work out a strategy to accomplish a successful workplace transition. In my case, I was very fortunate to have my future wife as a confidante and sounding board. I was also able to draw on the advice of my therapist and the "mature" transgender support group that she ran, as well as my new friend Aejaie who I mentioned previously is the proprietor of Carla's Social Club, a discreet and private place where transgender people and the cross-dressing community can gather and shop.

It is difficult to predict how anyone will react to your news about your intention to transition. What I have found to be the best indication of support or acceptance is whether they are members of the LGBTQ+ community or close to anyone who is. In my case, I received very strong support from family members who were familiar with LGBTQ+ issues, and older friends (from pre-transition life) and newer friends (after beginning the transition) who were part of the LGBTQ+ community. These individuals have a deep knowledge about the process of self-discovery and coming out and have empathy for those who are facing these issues.

As you begin to think about who you can enlist to support you, do so in the context of deciding who you can confide in, avoiding guilt or shame, without worrying about how they may react or what they think. You are not doing anything wrong or are somehow inadequate; you are having the courage to live your truth.

In deciding who to tell, try to be as analytical as possible. One way to approach decision-making is by creating a checklist that will identify the key information required to assess the issues which could impact how your chosen individuals can best support you. The questions below can help sort out the different aspects of your existing relationships and inform your decision as to whether to enlist them as allies during your transition.

The checklist: who can I count on for advice or moral support?

Family/Friends: spouse, ex-spouse, children, parents, siblings, extended family, friends from your pre-transition life, friends from your new life, your therapist, or other healthcare provider may all be considered as potential allies. Note that I have not included friends from your workplace. I have found that it is best to make your intention to transition as complete and consistent as possible, and you'll learn much more about this in Chapter 4. Although you may have friends and even an LGBTQ+ support group at work who you may consider enlisting for support, my advice is that if you disclose your intentions to co-workers at this early stage you run the risk of being inadvertently outed before you are ready. However, these allies in the office will be crucial to your post-transition success.

Questions to consider:

1. Should I tell my partner or spouse?

    a. How long have you been together?

b. How strong would you consider your relationship to be with your partner with respect to commitment, loyalty, and empathy?

c. Has your partner been aware of your cross-dressing or even participated in role play with you?

d. How accepting has your partner been and has the acceptance changed over time?

e. If there has never been a discussion with your partner, do you think he or she suspects that you may be transgender?

f. Do you think your partner is progressive or open-minded enough to understand and potentially support a transition?

2. Should I tell other family members?

   a. Children

      i. Are your children old enough to understand and support your decision?

      ii. Do your children live with you?

      iii. How close are you to your children?

      iv. Are your children familiar with the concept of gender non-conformity, and do they know other gender non-conforming people?

      v. Are your children aware of your identity questions?

      vi. How close are your children with your spouse?

   b. Parents

      i. Are your parents or step-parents alive?

      ii. Are you close to them?

      iii. How progressive or open-minded are they?

    iv. Do their religious beliefs pose a potential issue?

    v. Do they know any gender non-conforming people or others in the LGBTQ+ community?

    vi. Have they expressed any positions on gender non-conformity or gay marriage?

3. Should I tell friends from my pre-trans life?

    a. Are they members of the LGBTQ+ community?

    b. How progressive or open-minded are they?

    c. Do their religious beliefs pose a potential issue?

    d. Do they know any gender non-conforming people or others in the LGBTQ+ community?

    e. Have they expressed any positions on gender non-conformity or marriage equality?

    f. Are they connected at all to your workplace or could their inadvertent disclosure of your situation bleed over to your work?

4. Should I tell my friends or support group members from my new trans life?

    a. Will new transgender friends and/or their friends be able to help you?

    b. Are they connected to or aware of your family or work situation beyond what you tell them?

    c. Are they in a similar business or employment situation to you?

    d. Are they in a similar family situation to you?

In general, this group can be expected to be supportive but may be on a very different social, work, or economic plane from you, and usually will not know much if anything about your prior life or the people in your family aside from what you have shared with them. But in many cases, they can provide their own experiences and reassurance about how their transition went and have insight as to some of the key events and challenges they faced.

5. Can I count on my therapist/healthcare practitioner for more than in-office professional support?

I believe that it is important to keep this relationship strictly professional. Your therapist will always be supportive and provide advice, lists of resources for every aspect of your transition, and examples from what has happened with other clients without violating their confidentiality. Many therapists, like mine, run support groups for transgender individuals and families. However, I don't recommend asking for personal help outside the bounds of that relationship, and most therapists would not cross into that role.

Be strong

Once you gain insight into how other people may take your news, and you get a few positive and supportive reactions under your belt, you can begin to build up a bit of resilience for having these conversations. However difficult they may be, do not let that dissuade you once you decide to transition. The goal of this chapter has been to help you reduce or limit the number of surprises and disappointments you might face.

The hardest part of these conversations is to stay as neutral and calm as possible, and to not let your emotions drive the conversation to a point where you regret things you've said or done. The best way to avoid that regret is to look at each relationship analytically and to give yourself the space to thoroughly and systematically explore all the decisions you will have to make.

As you move forward with your transition, you will want to identify where and from whom you can expect to get support. Your resilience can be bolstered by surrounding yourself with positivity, and that means people who have your back. You want to try to minimize the fallout from anyone who is going to be negative, because you have a long road ahead.

Remember, you're not the only one who is changing. You're not the only one who is transitioning. All the people in your orbit have to make an adjustment. Some are going to have to make bigger changes than others. Some you will be able to have more gravitational pull on, including your children and your spouse or partner. The more thought you can put into the decision-making and the conversations beforehand, the less regret you'll have afterwards because you're giving it the greatest opportunity to succeed the first time.

CHAPTER 2

CHARTING YOUR MEDICAL FUTURE

Whether you are transitioning from male to female (MTF), or female to male (FTM), you will have many choices for your medical and surgical transition. It is beyond the scope of this book to review the details of each procedure. My intention is to provide an overview of options so that you can choose those that are most appropriate for you, create a timeline for implementing therapies and surgeries, and lay out the best practices from a medical perspective.

The medical aspects of transition are some of the most emotionally and physically challenging parts of a very complicated process. For many, this is the final step to becoming the person you have always wanted to be. In my case, when I realized that I needed to transition, I wanted it to happen as fast as possible, and it was very hard to be patient and allow myself enough time to learn about my options and the implications of all the decisions. I kept thinking that I wished I had transitioned earlier and I wanted to make up for lost time. This sense of urgency, combined with high emotion, can lead to making a rushed decision, without fully understanding all the risks and complications of a particular choice. Ultimately, I'm glad I took the time to think things through and planned a timeline that worked for my job and for me.

It can also be a nerve-racking time, since you may not yet be out to your family, your co-workers, or your current doctors. There is an understandable fear of being outed or discovered even as you begin to explore the options or consult with new medical providers. Or, you may not be out to anyone apart from your medical providers, so there may be an additional fear of disclosure, either to family or at the workplace by accessing healthcare insurance benefits provided by your employer. These insurance benefits and all the details of your medical care are supposed to be confidential but the understandable fear remains about either inadvertent disclosure by a provider or their office staff, or possibly being seen visiting the office of a known provider of transgender care. However, I want to assure you that qualified providers will always be sensitive to your privacy, your unique situation, and will try to tailor a transition plan that fits your physical, emotional, and financial needs.

Lastly, the medical and surgical aspects of the physical changes can be extensive, and the recovery can be protracted and uncomfortable, so you need to be prepared. You need to understand the details of all the medical and surgical choices and plan for your convalescence.

Building your team: finding the right providers

In the same way that it is important to connect early with the right therapist, a healthy and productive provider/patient relationship will be crucial to your success. The reality is that a physical transition can take years to be fully realized, and your doctors need to be a constant resource for you. They should be able to completely evaluate your pre-transition health status, and then discuss your goals and the likely outcomes for each procedure or medical therapy.

Depending on which decisions you make regarding how you want to transition, your path will be very individualized. Your doctors should clearly discuss the benefits and risks of any medical treatments or surgical procedures, many of which are highly complex with extensive recovery times and commitments for aftercare. They should be able to address any questions or hesitations without pressure or coercion and allow you to take more time to make a decision, especially for irrevocable procedures like gender reassignment surgery (GRS). In my case, I decided to do the more cosmetic procedures first, including facial feminization and "top" surgery, and it took me over two-and-a-half years to make the final decision to move forward with the gender reassignment "bottom" surgery.

The minimum initial treatment team should include a mental health provider knowledgeable in gender dysphoria and the mental health concerns of transition, a primary care provider able to deliver appropriate care for regular medical issues as well as those relevant to transgender patients, and potentially a medical provider knowledgeable in transgender hormone therapy, such as an endocrinologist. Your primary practitioner can also do the hormone prescriptions, but you may need an endocrine specialist if your previous health status indicates it is necessary, or if your primary provider is not comfortable prescribing hormones.

An experienced plastic surgeon will be necessary for facial feminization procedures (MTF) and top surgery (both MTF and FTM), and a team consisting of a plastic surgeon and a urologic surgeon is usually required for gender reassignment surgery (bottom surgery for both MTF and FTM).

When looking for a doctor, the first consideration should be to find one who is empathetic and who believes that it is not only ethical, but necessary, to treat transgender patients in ways that alter body structures and functions. According to the World Professional Association for Transgender Health (WPATH) Standards of Care:

> In ordinary surgical practice, pathological tissues are removed to restore disturbed functions, or alterations are made to body features to improve a patient's self-image. Some people, including some health professionals, object on ethical grounds to surgery

as a treatment for gender dysphoria, because these conditions are thought not to apply.[1]

If your doctor believes transgender care is not ethical, no matter how "wonderful" they are or how long your therapeutic relationship has been, it's time to find another doctor. You want your doctor to be on the same moral plane with you, and you must find someone who is caring and thoughtful about what you're going through. They are out there and, if you persevere, I guarantee that there will be somebody who is right for you.

It is also important to seek medical treatment, especially concerning hormones, from a provider who has experience and training specifically in the care of transgender patients. Dr. Renee McLaughlin, a senior medical director and market executive, is a transgender physician employee of the health insurance company, Cigna. Renee is an expert in insurance coverage for LGBTQ+ patients. She sees the biggest challenge for patients as the access to well-trained, well-informed healthcare professionals. Her view is reflected in recent data published in a 2017 letter in the *Journal of the American Medical Association*,[2] which shows that nearly 75 percent of practicing primary care physicians in the military have no training in transgender care. However, in endocrinology, the research is more promising, with nearly 75 percent of endocrinology fellowship program directors stating that they provide teaching in transgender medicine, and over 90 percent stating that transgender medicine training is important.

For instance, Antonia, the transgender woman mentioned in Chapter 1, wanted to start taking female hormones right away and

---

1   *Standards of Care for the Health of Transsexual, Transgender, and Gender Nonconforming People*, V7 (2011) p.55. The World Professional Association for Transgender Health. Available at https://s3.amazonaws.com/amo_hub_content/Association140/files/Standards%20of%20Care%20V7%20-%202011%20WPATH%20(2)(1).pdf.
2   *JAMA Internal Medicine* (2017), 177, 5, 727–729. doi: 10.1001/jamainternmed.2017.0136. Available at https://jamanetwork.com/journals/jamainternalmedicine/fullarticle/10.1001/jamainternmed.2017.0136.

was put in touch with a doctor who was recommended by some of her trans friends. At the time, she felt it was a safe decision to see this new provider because she didn't want to involve her regular family doctor who might tell her wife before Antonia was ready to disclose. The new doctor prescribed hormones, but within six months she had high levels of prolactin. When she asked her doctor what these high levels meant, the doctor responded, "Well, I don't really know; I'm not really a specialist in this type of thing." This doctor was a caring provider, but had no business prescribing hormones.

The next doctor she found was highly regarded and a leader in the transgender medical field in England. When Antonia found the right care, she learned that the combination of oestrogen therapy with some male hormone blockers can lead to high prolactin levels, which is found in some types of tumors. The new doctor modified her hormones to reduce prolactin levels. Clearly, a knowledgeable provider is very important.

If you absolutely cannot find the right providers, you may have to be proactive in educating your current physician. This would require becoming very familiar with the guidelines for transgender healthcare, as provided by the WPATH or the Endocrine Society. Sending your doctor an email or text with the links to these resources can help if they are not familiar with them. I have always found that the time in the doctor's office is very limited, and it is helpful to take your time when you are at home or in a quiet place to read through all the material so that you can fully appreciate what lies ahead.

Of course, a physician who is unfamiliar must be empathetic to your needs and receptive to learning about transgender care from you. In addition, your providers may connect you with websites or support groups for individuals contemplating procedures and other treatments for a transition.

In the US, high-quality transgender healthcare can be obtained in many large cities, such as San Francisco, Los Angeles, Chicago, Boston, and New York, and medical centers at many major research universities. Dr. Asa Radix works at Callen-Lorde Community Health

Center in New York City. He is the Senior Director of Research and Education and the center has treated over 4400 transgender patients. Dr. Radix, who has degrees in medicine and public health and is a specialist in infectious diseases and HIV medicine, started working with the transgender community in 1990 as a primary care provider. Prior to any surgical procedure, he recommends interviewing two surgeons if possible, just to get a good feel for the surgeons and to assess their "bedside manner." His practice also hosts a facilitated, drop-in support group for people contemplating transgender surgery. Other providers can be found through the TransHealthCare Surgeon Directory (www.transhealthcare.org).

Recently, telemedicine—the use of telecommunication and information technology to provide clinical healthcare from a distance—is becoming a high-level option for patients who cannot get quality care where they live. This may be particularly helpful for transgender individuals who live outside big cities. Medical practices like QueerMed.com have been established and QueerMed.com has as its mission "affirming healthcare and hormone therapy for the trans community." A preliminary internet search shows a handful of telemedicine options across the country. Some are licensed in a few states, and others can see patients across a region. For example, QueerMed.com, which is based in Atlanta, Georgia, currently only treats patients who reside in the Southern US—Alabama, Georgia, North Carolina, South Carolina, and Tennessee.

All telemedicine practices utilize video conference software and personal visits if necessary. Patients then use local laboratories for blood tests and pharmacies to fill prescriptions. Telemedicine is covered under many insurance plans, making this a viable and affordable option that highlights speed.

How to talk to a doctor

The same conversational approach and tone you use to ensure a good relationship with a therapist is needed for your doctors. The most important thing to remember is to be open and honest with all of your providers. Don't be afraid to explain your needs and answer their questions completely: there is no right or wrong thing you can say. They are bound by confidentiality and routinely help patients maintain their privacy. Nearly all the medical care providers I spoke with expressed how important it was for patients to be comfortable and unafraid of being outed.

Dr. Rachel Bluebond-Langner is Associate Professor of Reconstructive Plastic Surgery in the Hansjörg Wyss Department of Plastic Surgery at NYU Langone Health and specializes in a combination of gender-affirming surgery and general reconstructive surgery, including facial feminization. She told me that many of her patients who first come to see her are anxious and afraid of being misunderstood. They are also worried that if they say the wrong thing they will not qualify for care under their insurance policy, or that she will choose not to perform a particular procedure. Her advice is to be completely honest. The doctors in this field will not judge you; they are here to help you achieve the best possible outcome.

The American Society of Plastic Surgeons created an authoritative report with suggestions about what makes a qualified surgeon.[3] The following are important questions to discuss with your surgeon, regardless of the procedure. Make sure you are comfortable with their answers:

- What kind of training do you have?

- Are you board certified in plastic surgery?

- How long have you been caring for transgender patients?

- How many of these surgeries have you done?

- Are you pursuing continuing medical education in this specialty?

- What complications may arise?

---

3   www.plasticsurgery.org/patient-safety?sub=Questions+to+ask+your+plastic+ surgeon.

- Will you be available after the surgery and going forward for consultations or revisions if necessary?

- Will I get reports back from you about the details of the procedure and any complications that may have occurred in the operating room?

- How easy is it for me to contact you if I have an issue or complications?

- Do you have photographs of successful operations? If so, will you require my consent to take photographs of me? How do you intend to use these photographs?

- When is your next availability? A word of caution here: if there is a surgeon who can take you tomorrow, and there is no waiting list, it is not a good sign. The best surgeons are booked a year or more in advance, although cancellations happen and you might be able to get in earlier if you are proactive (and lucky). It can be very disheartening to wait so long for a scheduled procedure, but there may be things you can do in the meantime to improve your outcome, like have additional hair removal before GRS or a longer course of oestrogen which can enable a better outcome for MTF top surgery. Before you know it, the time for surgery will arrive.

USE THE INTERNET AS A RESOURCE

Online groups like Transbucket, or transgender Facebook groups, may feature photographs of surgeries and medical recommendations.

Developing your wish list and timeline

If you are seeking care for gender dysphoria, there are many therapeutic options that can be considered. The number and type of interventions applied and the order in which these take place may differ from person to person. However, while the fact that you've decided to medically transition is incredibly liberating, it can also cause anxiety, impatience, and frustration, and an unwillingness to go through a set timeline or follow a provider's advice. Dr. Radix told me, "There are folks who've been thinking for a long time about their transition who come in saying, 'I need my hormones yesterday.'"

Yet the truth is, no matter how ready you are, you can't rush the process. It takes time to line up the right appointments and surgeries. Every step is an important one, and keeping the momentum going, and moving forward with the right guidance are key to having the most successful outcomes.

A carefully considered timeline also allows for the mental space to think through and become comfortable with the realization of what each surgery entails, and how it will affect your overall well-being. Slowing down the pace of these surgical procedures may also ensure that the social and psychological aspects of your transition align with the changes to your appearance. In addition, the availability and extent of insurance coverage or financial resources can influence your transition path.

The following is a suggestion for a best practice timeline that can be applied to MTF or FTM procedures.

Start by accessing mental health support

If you haven't done so already, you must get a mental health therapist on board. A licensed clinical social worker, psychologist, or psychiatrist is needed to create an assessment letter that attests to the potential diagnosis of gender dysphoria and overall mental health status before a surgical procedure. They can also help prepare you mentally for hormone therapy as well as surgery, and support you prior to surgery and post-surgery.

I was a bit leery about a letter and what it might say, but it is actually the key to accessing many services and procedures, as well as insurance coverage. The intent of the letter is to show that the surgery is necessary for your care, so that is why insurance companies require it. In some cases, you may need two letters, especially for GRS.

According to the WPATH guidelines, the recommended content of the referral letter for feminizing/masculinizing hormone therapy and/or surgery is as follows:

1. The client's general identifying characteristics.

2. Results of the client's psychosocial assessment, including any diagnoses.

3. The duration of the referring health professional's relationship with the client, including the type of evaluation and therapy or counseling to date.

4. An explanation that the criteria for hormone therapy or surgery have been met, and a brief description of the clinical rationale for supporting the client's request.

5. A statement about the fact that informed consent has been obtained from the patient.

6. A statement that the referring health professional is available for coordination of care and welcomes a phone call to establish this.

As we discussed in the previous chapter, the therapeutic fit of the referring mental health professional is incredibly important, and you need to ensure that you have somebody who has experience, and is someone with whom you can feel comfortable and confident in being honest and open about your experiences.

Gender-affirming therapies: hormones

Hormone therapy is usually the first step to beginning the physical process of a transition for many reasons and can be prescribed by your primary care doctor or an endocrinologist. According to the WPATH guidelines, feminizing/masculinizing hormone therapy is a medically necessary intervention for many transgender people and gender non-conforming individuals with gender dysphoria. Some people seek maximum feminization or masculinization, while others find relief at the point when they have created an androgynous expression.

A prescribing clinician must first confirm the diagnostic criteria of gender dysphoria before beginning hormone treatment, and hormone therapies should begin only after a complete physical to make sure that there are no other underlying problems that could be affected or cause complications.

Approval for gender-affirming surgeries typically takes place only after completion of at least one year of consistent and compliant hormone treatment. These guidelines were adopted to ensure that people are absolutely certain they're ready to make the transition. However, more recent guidelines are less stringent and allow for some flexibility. If a patient is not suited for hormone therapy or refuses it, they can still be considered for surgery with recommendations from mental health providers.

For FTM transitions, progestins are used to assist with menstrual cessation, and testosterone is used to grow facial hair, lower the voice, and build muscle. Testosterone is delivered as an intramuscular injection or a cream that you put on your skin. The cream is slightly problematic because it can cross-contaminate others in your household and may then inadvertently lead to unwanted side effects for a partner or family member.

Another issue regarding testosterone is that it is considered to be a "Schedule III drug" by the United States Drug Enforcement Administration, which means that it is highly regulated and has the potential for abuse. Schedule I drugs are those which have no therapeutic use in the US, like heroin, LSD or ecstasy. Schedule II drugs do have some therapeutic uses in the US but carry a potential for abuse, such as methadone, OxyContin, and fentanyl. Other examples of drugs besides anabolic steroids that are Schedule III are combination narcotic painkillers with hydrocodone, such as

Vicodin, or combinations of acetaminophen with codeine. Due to this Schedule III designation, a pharmacy will not refill a prescription until the exact time elapses from the previous one. This is a consequence of steroid abuse by athletes, and it makes obtaining hormones for trans men much more difficult than for trans women. It can be particularly problematic if you are planning to be on vacation or out of the country when you need a refill, since only a limited supply can be provided with every prescription.

For MTF individuals, hormonal treatments include oestrogen, progestins (not always necessary), as well as androgen or testosterone blockers. Oestrogen and progestin are usually delivered as a patch, which can sometimes cause a rash or not adhere to the skin for the required number of days. It is recommended that hormone levels are monitored so that they approximate those of a genetic female but it is challenging to predict which type of patch is best and it may take some time to achieve the right doses. Some providers prescribe long-acting implants of oestrogens, but again, getting the right levels is a challenge.

According to the Clinical Practice Guidelines for the Endocrine Treatment of Gender-Dysphoric/Gender-Incongruent Persons, endocrinologists are the specialist doctors who can develop a hormonal program tailored to your specific needs. Your chosen internist or endocrinologist needs to work in collaboration with your mental health provider to create the best treatment plan for you. Another option for exploring hormone treatment is with the doctors and other medical professionals at your local Planned Parenthood clinic. The website (www.plannedparenthood.org) lists this service under the heading "LGBT Services."

There are places on the internet where you may be able to acquire hormones without a doctor's supervision, which is very different from participating in telemedicine, which does have a doctor's involvement. As described in a 2016 article in *The Atlantic*,[4]

---

4   www.theatlantic.com/health/archive/2016/08/diy-hormone-replacement-therapy/498044.

there are online forums and blogs that are devoted to do-it-yourself hormone replacement therapies (also known as DIY-HRT) that help transgender people access drugs that are meant to be obtained only by a doctor's prescription and delivered from certified pharmacies. The members of these websites recommend online pharmacies of dubious legality in terms of the actual prescription and shipping and possession of such drugs. The patients who utilize these DIY sites monitor their own blood results and manage each other's side effects—all without the oversight of a doctor. *The Atlantic* article goes on to say:

> According to Libby Baney, executive director of the Alliance for Safe Online Pharmacies and a lawyer specializing in the regulation of the healthcare supply chain, patients are rolling the dice when they order prescription medications or controlled substances through most online pharmacies. There is the possibility that these pharmacies are selling counterfeit medicine… Even if the drugs are legitimate and not counterfeit, many of these pharmacies and manufacturers do not have the same safety standards as the FDA [Food and Drug Administration] and the US government, as the medications can come from India, Russia, and Pakistan. (All Day Chemist, an online pharmacy based in India, even has a strict "as-is" policy, meaning they do not claim 100 percent certainty about the products they sell.) Hormones manufactured and distributed from abroad might be contaminated, or kept out of cold storage, which is necessary to keep them from degrading. "Even if you're lucky enough not to get a counterfeit, you don't know the quality of the medicine you get," Baney says.

This is troublesome for a variety of reasons. While you may not yet be comfortable talking about your plans with your existing doctor or are worried that your private medical information will work its way back to your office, these concerns should not lead you to make a decision without medical guidance that will affect your health in the long term. The bottom line is that hormone therapy is not for everybody and needs to be closely monitored by a professional. It is serious medicine and can lead to significant side effects like blood clots and liver damage for oestrogen therapy, or high red blood cell counts, liver damage, and psychiatric problems for testosterone therapy. There may also be interactions with other medications you may be taking for pre-existing conditions that might not make hormones a wise choice. Hormone levels need to be delicately balanced and require constant monitoring to avoid cancer risks, cardiovascular issues, loss of bone density, and diabetes.

Oral hormone therapy passes through the digestive tract into the liver, which is why most therapies are either injections or transdermal creams or patches. If you take too much it can cause all sorts of damage. So again, if you are uncomfortable talking about your real health issues with your existing internist or primary care physician, it's time to find a new one, or add an endocrinologist to your team.

When hormones are prescribed, they are used to develop the physical characteristics of the intended gender. Hormone treatments can both suppress your original sex hormone secretion and maintain sex hormone levels within the normal range for your desired gender. Some people seek maximum feminization or masculinization, while others experience relief of their gender dysphoria with an androgynous or gender fluid presentation resulting from hormonal minimization of existing sex characteristics. Transgender patients will need lifelong therapy so it is important to get the right balance to obtain the benefits with minimal side effects.

The physical changes that come with hormone therapy are usually accompanied by an improvement in mental well-being. For me, there was an immediate gratification when I started taking hormones. When I first realized I was transgender, my psychologist referred me to my wonderful internist, and I wanted to start hormones that day. The truth is, I'm a licensed physician, and I could have written the prescription for myself. However, I accepted my therapist's advice and sought a licensed provider who was experienced in transgender health, and who would be completely objective, empathetic to my gender situation and provide the comprehensive care I needed. Even though her initial examination, the blood tests, and the wait to receive the results seemed endless, it was all necessary. For her to follow accepted medical practice prior to writing the prescription, she required a comprehensive background examination and a complete understanding of my current medical condition. Once I was cleared, and I applied my first oestrogen patch and took the blockers for the testosterone, I immediately felt that I was a major step closer to being the real me.

I wasn't prepared for the moodiness that accompanied taking female hormones. They also affected my work, as I was occasionally irritable, fatigued, and lost my patience. At first, I didn't realize that sometimes I was acting like a complete jerk, but after a month, it finally dawned on me that my new higher oestrogen levels were causing the same symptoms as premenstral syndrome.

TABLE 2.1: MASCULINIZING EFFECTS OF HORMONES FOR TRANSGENDER MALES

Effect	Onset of change in months	Maximum effect delivered in years
Skin oiliness/acne	1–6	1–2
Facial/body hair growth	6–12	4–5
Scalp hair loss	6–12	Treatment is the same as with biological men
Increased muscle mass/strength	6–12	2–5
Fat redistribution	1–6	2–5
Cessation of menses	1–6	Heavy bleeding requires gynecology assessment
Clitoral enlargement	1–6	1–2
Vaginal atrophy	1–6	1–2
Deepening of voice	6–12	1–2

TABLE 2.2: FEMINIZING EFFECTS OF HORMONES FOR TRANSGENDER FEMALES

Effect	Onset of change in months	Maximum effect delivered in years
Redistribution of body fat	3–6	2–3
Decrease in muscle mass and strength	3–6	1–2
Softening of skin/decreased oiliness	3–6	Unknown
Decreased sexual desire	1–3	.25–.5
Decreased spontaneous erections	1–3	.25–.5
Male sexual dysfunction	Variable	Variable
Breast growth	3–6	2–3
Decreased testicular volume	3–6	2–3
Decreased sperm production	Unknown	>3
Decreased terminal hair growth	6–12	>3
Scalp hair	Variable	Genetic hair loss may occur if oestrogen therapy is stopped
Voice	None	Treatment by speech pathologists is most effective

Gender-affirming surgeries

I believe that all surgeries related to a transition are gender affirming, regardless of where on the body they take place. These include facial feminization, "top surgery," which refers to breast implants or mastectomy, and "bottom surgery" or gender reassignment. Some of the surgeries are reversible, such as breast implants, or subtle, such as facial feminization. Gender reassignment (genital surgery) is irreversible.

Medical decisions about transitioning are completely indivi-dualized—whether or not you elect to have specific surgeries or therapies is directly related to how you feel about your body and how you need to look in order to be your most authentic self. Your existing anatomy may set your priorities list. For example, some people don't need to have facial surgery if they have a fairly androgynous face.

Once I decided to address my dysphoria surgically, then my wish list came into place fairly quickly.

Everyone's wish list will be different. For example, the following statistics from a 2011 report entitled *Injustice at Every Turn: A Report of the National Transgender Discrimination Survey* show the prevalence of the most common surgeries and therapies.[5]

MTF

- Hormone therapy: 62 percent have had, 23 percent want (includes MTF and FTM).

- Breast augmentation: 21 percent have had, 53 percent want.

- Orchiectomy (removal of testicles): 25 percent have had, 61 percent want.

- Vaginoplasty (construction of a vagina): 23 percent have had, 64 percent want.

- Facial feminization: while there is no data available, it is relatively common and covers a wide range of procedures.

FTM

- Mastectomy (removal of breasts): 43 percent have had, 50 percent want.

- Hysterectomy (removal of uterus): 21 percent have had, 58 percent want.

- Metoidioplasty (enlarging the clitoris to simulate a penis): 4 percent have had, 53 percent want.

- Phalloplasty (construction of a penis): 2 percent have had, 27 percent want.

---

5   Grant, J.M., Mottet, L.A., Tanis, J., Harrison, J., Herman, J.L., and Keisling, M. (2011) *Injustice at Every Turn: A Report of the National Transgender Discrimination Survey.* Washington: National Center for Transgender Equality and National Gay and Lesbian Task Force, p.79.

I wanted to do facial feminization first, because I thought it would represent a real difference from my prior male appearance and it is the most apparent feature to others. The next thing I wanted was breasts. The last thing, which was more private and irreversible, and requires the most time for recovery and aftercare, is genital surgery.

While the timeline and wish list you develop are important, your doctor's schedule may dictate some of your decision-making. There are a limited number of qualified surgeons who do these complicated procedures, although their numbers and locations are increasing. However, if they are good, they are often incredibly busy, and you may have to wait months for a consultation, then many more months to be scheduled for the procedure. When I tried to book my "bottom surgery," I informed my local surgeon in November, and the earliest he could get me into the calendar was the following September. I didn't want to wait that long so found another excellent surgeon but had to travel across the country to have the procedure. In addition, some procedures require extensive convalescence, while others do not. The amount of time you need to recover and get back to work after surgery will also influence the timing of your next procedure.

Outside the US, government-controlled healthcare can also influence your timeline. For example, Stuart Barette, who lives in the UK, wanted to transition from female to male. He told me that had he relied only on public insurance from the limited number of qualified providers in the National Health Service, his transition would have required a four-year wait for his referral to go through the UK healthcare system. He told me, "By the time you get to the front of the queue, then you have to actually have two separate appointments nine months apart because of the waiting list, just to get your diagnosis [of gender dysphoria]. Then it would take another four months to be able to start hormones. Luckily, I was able to go privately for my diagnosis and my hormones. I had them within 18 months of starting my social transition. However, the government won't allow you to go privately for any parts of the surgery unless you are paying for all of the surgery, so because I couldn't afford the lower surgery, they insisted that I went with them for the whole piece. By the time I got my second sign off and it had gone into the queue for the surgeon, it took an entire year to see the doctor and schedule the surgery. So if I hadn't been able to go private for some of my treatments, just the top surgery would have taken around five years. Right now, the wait for lower surgery through the public system is seven years, finishing in ten years' time."

Your timeline will provide the structure for many of your decisions regarding transitioning at work, because you will need to factor in taking time off for the surgery and recovery. I recommend that you tell your boss, and your HR department (if you have one), about your transition before you embark on any surgery. You may need to schedule your procedures around sick leave, vacation days and holidays. If your employer is covering these procedures through its health insurance plan, you may be able to take a medical or disability leave of absence and continue to receive at least partial pay.

Facial feminization surgery

Depending on your own anatomy, facial surgery can entail, as it did with me, fairly significant restructuring of cheek bones, eye sockets, brow, nose, jaw, and chin. A second, more cosmetic part of facial surgery, can include a facelift, eyelid reconstruction (blepharoplasty), fat grafts, enhancement of the lips, cheeks or the chin, changes in the nose, and a tracheal shave or reduction in the size of the Adam's apple. Both of these rounds of surgery require approximately six months to heal, meaning a year or more for the complete process and recovery. There's a lot of bruising and swelling and many people feel that they're not presentable for a month or more after each stage.

I wasn't prepared for how uncomfortable the recovery from facial surgery was going to be. The first surgery involved modifying the bones of my brow, eye sockets and cheeks, so there was significant deep pain and swelling. Also, my nostrils were reshaped and my jaw and chin were modified. I was fortunate that they didn't have to break my nasal bones.

When I woke up in the hospital after the 13-hour procedure, my entire upper face was bandaged and I couldn't see—it was frightening! The bandage came off after two days, but I did not expect to be completely blind when I woke up. It took three weeks for the bruising to subside, but probably the most discomfort was around my nose. Until the stitches were removed seven days later, it was extremely uncomfortable and I couldn't breathe through my nose.

Seven months later I started phase two for my face, which was more cosmetic but also involved another 13 hours of surgery for the meticulous processes of a facelift, blepharoplasties (reconstruction of the eyelids), fat grafts to my cheeks, fat grafts into my lips and further modification of my chin. Although this did not cause the deep pain I endured after the bony restructuring, it was excruciatingly uncomfortable since there were stitches all around my eyes and metal surgical staples and stitches from the back of my ears all around my hairline. It took over four hours in the surgeon's office just to remove the stitches and staples, but I was much more comfortable afterwards.

Breast and chest surgery

Plastic surgeons are well versed in this routine surgery that either removes existing breasts or creates new ones. MTF transitions can include breast augmentation, which involves inserting silicone or other types of prostheses beneath the chest muscles. This surgery takes a few hours and does not usually require an overnight stay in the hospital. I was back to work the next day because of an important meeting that had been scheduled for some time, but I had significant discomfort, and the decision to return to work the next day is one I would not make if I could do it again. Instead, I recommend scheduling this surgery for a Thursday or Friday and then taking a long weekend to recover, so that you can get back to work on Monday.

For the trans masculine patient, the procedure is called chest masculinization. This will include a breast reduction or mastectomy, followed by reconstruction. There are four types of top surgery for trans men. If you've got small breasts to start with, there are two types that get good results and are usually recommended, and there are two types that work best for trans men with larger chests. One important factor is whether your existing nipples are very large and can be resized to look like a natural male nipple, and whether the normal sensitivity can be retained. The reconstruction can be quite challenging, especially the modification of the nipples. This is much more difficult than it seems, and some surgeons require a couple of revisions to get it right once the swelling goes down after the initial mastectomy.

Genital and gender reassignment surgery, MTF

For both MTF and FTM surgeries, there are external and visible aspects, and then an internal aspect that requires significant changes with respect to urination. Each one of these procedures has varying degrees of difficulty, including the technical parts of the operations as well as the recovery, and how you should prepare for these surgeries.

Vaginoplasty includes the deconstruction of the penis, the removal of the corporeal tissue and the testicles, and then the creation of the vagina, labia and clitoris. It can be done in a single operation, which usually lasts four or five hours, depending on the anatomy. The tip of the glans of the penis becomes the clitoris. The urethra is shortened, and the extra urethral tissue is used to line the vulva so that when you spread the labia you see pink. A vaginal canal is created between the rectum and the prostate. The penile and scrotal skin are used to line the vaginal cavity. Surgeons usually aim for six inches of depth, which gets you to basically the peritoneal reflection, which may be the anatomic limit for the vaginal canal. The post-operative stage for vaginoplasty is an enormous commitment, requiring daily dilation of the new vagina to eventually create a large enough opening for intercourse and to prevent closure. For the first month, dilation is recommended four times a day for 15 minutes, then three times daily for the second month and then twice daily thereafter. Although I knew that dilation was necessary, I didn't realize that it can sometimes be a challenge to work it into your daily routine, especially when it is more than twice a day. For those who are going back to work, you need to be able to find a private place to dilate during that second month, like a room which is set aside for new mothers who are pumping breast milk.

There is another surgical option for MTF which only entails creation of external female genitalia without a vagina, called a zero-depth vulvoplasty. This includes removing the penis and testicles, and creates a clitoris and vulva, but no vagina. It is a shorter procedure and the recovery is quicker and does not require dilation. However, it precludes vaginal sex, so you need to be sure you won't ever want to have vaginal penetrating sex before you choose this option. If that is not important to you, then you don't need to have the more complex surgery.

If you are having a vaginoplasty, surgeons have to create the new vaginal canal and also ensure that the bladder and urethra function normally. It is very different urinating without the penis, and the bladder control takes getting used to. Men are used to having a valve or sphincter below the bladder and another one at the base of the penis, which prevents unwanted urine from escaping. Women only have a single valve so it takes some getting used to in order to completely control the bladder emptying after the vaginoplasty.

Genital and gender reassignment surgery, FTM

According to Dr. Rachel Bluebond-Langner, phalloplasty has many more steps, can take up to a year to complete, requiring two if not three or four operations. Fewer trans men come in for genital reconstruction compared to trans women due to the extensive commitment for multiple procedures and the higher complication rates. Prior to the genital surgery, most FTM patients have a total oophorectomy and hysterectomy, which is the removal of the ovaries and uterus.

After that operation, the gender reassignment procedures include removal of the vagina, lengthening of the urethra, and creating a penis and testicles from tissue taken from the arm, back, or abdomen. When everything heals, which can take at least a year, a prosthesis can be added to the penis to achieve an erection.

A second option is called metoidioplasty or metaoidioplasty (informally referred to as a "meto" or "meta"). Testosterone replacement therapy gradually enlarges the clitoris, which is then used to simulate a penis. This technique is technically simpler than phalloplasty, costs less, and has fewer potential complications. Metoidioplasty typically requires two to three hours to complete, and because the erectile tissue of the clitoris continues to function, a prosthesis is unnecessary for achieving an erection.

Although both surgeries can seem daunting, it is becoming clear that medical and surgical advances are improving the outcomes for transgender surgeries, particularly GRS. According to Dr. Lee Zhao, a urologic surgeon at NYU Langone Health who specializes in repair and reconstruction of the urethra in transgender patients, only recently have there been organized symposia on transgender care for surgeons as part of general urology conferences. According to Dr. Zhao, we can expect to see more rapid improvements in transgender surgical success rates as the field advances. As someone who spent his career repairing poorly performed procedures, he is now pioneering the use of the latest technologies and practices, including the use of robotics during transgender surgery. His experience only underscores the need to find a competent provider who is as advanced as possible in the surgical treatments for transition.

Can I afford this? The insurance piece

By law, any medical procedure is completely confidential. However, a medically influenced transition may be hard to hide, and you need to know your rights and entitlements regarding insurance claims and the workplace, including planning medical or surgical leaves well in advance to provide sufficient notice to your employer.

Insurance coverage at work is completely dependent on the employer and sometimes your state of residence regarding what will be covered. For example, while there is better coverage of gender reassignment surgery and mastectomy for FTM trans people, there may not be coverage for what are deemed as cosmetic procedures, such as facial feminization and breast augmentation for MTF trans persons. There is a move among the most progressive companies, especially larger companies in technology and other sectors like Facebook and Intel, to cover everything that a doctor feels is medically necessary, including facial surgery, electrolysis, and even voice training. Read your policy carefully to determine what's covered, and what's not. For instance, the cost of assessment letters from mental health providers may not be covered. Many of these therapists don't even bill insurance these days because it's not worth it. If you're not covered by insurance and therefore have to pay for everything yourself, these letters may not be necessary for coverage. However, it may matter to the surgeon that somebody referred this patient and evaluated their mental state and suitability for the procedure as a hedge against any malpractice litigation.

Dr. Renee McLaughlin at Cigna says that she sees a steady increase in employers providing broader coverage. She told me, "I think right now coverage for GRS is like table stakes. I think hormone replacement therapy has also been well instilled into the basic benefit package. Where I'm seeing some real traction and a nice growth curve is in the coverage for other procedures, such as facial feminization, breast augmentation, and so on. I've seen a growing interest and willingness of employers, with the appropriate education—and that's a large part of it—to put coverage in place for those procedures. It's certainly not across the board, but the tech industry, entertainment industry, and legal industry are the most advanced now although it is expanding to many more. At Cigna we probably have close to a million customers who have now accessed coverage for those procedures."

What Medicare covers

Medicare is a US government insurance plan that covers older Americans and people with disabilities. In 2014, the prior exclusion for transgender surgery was eliminated for Medicare patients. This means that coverage-related decisions can now be made on an individual basis of medical need and the applicable standards of care, similar to other doctor or hospital coverage under Medicare. Medicare also covers medically necessary hormone therapies through Part D prescription drug lists.

Medicaid and the Affordable Care Act (ACA)

Medicaid is a public program in the US that provides health coverage for low-income individuals who fall into a range of eligibility categories, including people living with a disability, people who are pregnant, and people with dependent children. Eligibility is linked to individual or family income, and the program is required to cover all individuals who meet eligibility requirements. Medicaid is primarily administered by states within parameters set by federal law, and the program is jointly financed by states and the federal government— on average, the federal government pays 53 cents of every dollar spent by states on their Medicaid programs. With the Affordable Care Act passage, and its Medicaid expansion, by 2013, 22 percent of eligible LGBT+ people were insured by Medicaid, and by 2014 it had risen to 28 percent.

The Affordable Care Act (ACA) was passed in 2010 and is also known as "Obamacare." Section 1557 of the ACA is the health reform law's primary civil rights provision, and prohibits discrimination on the basis of race, color, national origin, disability, age, or sex by any program or entity that receives federal financial assistance.

Because every state Medicaid program receives financial support from the federal government, Section 1557 covers all Medicaid beneficiaries. Section 1557 has been in effect since the ACA was passed in 2010, but finally, in May 2016, the US Department of Health and Human Services Office for Civil Rights released regulations clarifying the scope and intent of Section 1557. Among other provisions, the final rule clarifies that Section 1557's sex-based non-discrimination protections extend to gender identity and sex stereotyping. Section 1557 thus explicitly protects transgender and gender non-conforming individuals and, while the regulations do not expressly define sexual orientation discrimination as a form of sex discrimination, they do protect gay, lesbian, and bisexual individuals and their families from discrimination on the basis of sex stereotypes. The final rule prohibits discriminatory design and marketing of plan benefits. It also prohibits health insurance coverage programs and plans from categorically excluding all services related to gender transition or making coverage decisions in a manner that results in discrimination against a transgender individual—such as denying coverage for mental health services related to gender transition while covering them for depression, among many other examples. It also requires healthcare providers to provide medically necessary healthcare services to transgender individuals, as long as those services are within the provider's scope of practice and are provided to non-transgender individuals. The provisions of the Section 1557 final rule took effect on July 18, 2016, for state Medicaid programs, meaning that the 18 states whose Medicaid programs still exclude transition-related care may face administrative remedies or private lawsuits if they do not remove these exclusions.

Medicaid is a state program and therefore eligibility and terms of coverage will vary from state to state. However, once you determine where your state exists in the provision of these options, you may be able to access transition-related services. For instance, New York is a state where gender-affirming surgery is covered.

Connecting coverage to a provider

Once you determine which therapies and procedures on your wish list are covered, then you have to determine if your provider of choice takes your insurance. This can be tricky in some locations and with some providers. According to psychiatrist Aron Janssen, his clinic in New York City doesn't accept insurance, but does provide services on a sliding scale. Another hospital associated with his practice does take insurance, and his team has admitting privileges there, so they can provide care in that setting.

However, I have met a number of dedicated providers who are very committed to providing transgender care and will accept all types of insurance and will assist patients in accessing the best coverage, even if they are initially uninsured. As you can imagine, if you don't have insurance, these procedures can be quite costly. Unfortunately, my company did not cover any transgender-related surgeries when I began my transition, so I had to pay for my facial surgeries and breast implants out of my savings, and it totaled nearly $100,000. Stuart Barette, who faced a ten-year wait to undergo gender-affirming surgery by going through the UK National Health Service, decided to take a lump sum severance payment from his company, which allowed him to pay privately for his procedure and drastically reduce the waiting time. So you may need to be creative to determine how you can access the funding for the care you need.

USING YOUR FLEXIBLE SPENDING ACCOUNT

If your insurance coverage is not completely comprehensive in covering what might be termed the more cosmetic procedures, such as electrolysis, your flexible spending account may cover some of the costs, but it is usually capped at around $2500 per year.

Consider a medical holiday: does the dollar go a long way in Thailand?

Many transitioning individuals opt out of the American healthcare system entirely. There are international centers, including "medical holiday" destinations like Thailand, which specialize in one-stop shopping for transgender surgeries.

Over the course of a month, individuals can have all of their needs met. People come from all over the world to have the same experience with a built-in support network. Dr. Asa Radix told me, "Patients are met at the airport. They're taken to a suite. They have the full medical pre-operative exam and clearance. They have their surgery. They recuperate and then they come back to the US. It's actually really great, especially for the people without the right health insurance coverage. You can do it all abroad for a few thousand dollars. If you tried to do it here it would cost you ten times more. However, there are many surgeons to choose from and you need to be careful that you are seeing the ones who are qualified, which can be difficult to assess. Some people may choose based on cost not competency, and like anywhere else, you can encounter people without good training. It can also be harder to evaluate qualifications overseas due to language barriers and differences in training requirements. Afterwards, people may experience complications when arriving home that are difficult to take care of. If things go wrong, patients may have no recourse or ability to get compensation. Lastly, it is difficult to go through surgeries without having your support systems of friends and family around you."

Surgery abroad still requires follow-up at home. You will still do your follow-up in the US—this is a long commitment and it requires ongoing treatment, just like any other condition. According to Dr. Radix, the patients he follows who have taken a medical holiday have generally been very pleased with the results. As he mentioned, the issue with a medical holiday is not the procedures, but the aftercare. If you have any problems or complications from the procedure, you can't be flown back to Thailand in an emergency.

Therefore, you should plan to have local medical/surgical support which can help if you run into problems when you get back; otherwise, you may need to access emergency rooms, which are not ideal places to provide this highly technical follow-up.

In the end, it's just the beginning

I consider myself to be very fortunate. I didn't have any insurance coverage from my employer for my early transition but I had the financial resources to accomplish everything on my wish list. However, new avenues are opening up to provide coverage through employers and the federal and state government. Even my old company finally changed its ways and offered coverage for transgender care in 2017.

Aydin Olson-Kennedy, MSW, Executive Director of the Los Angeles Gender Center, believes that once a person medically transitions they have to adjust to physically wearing their gender in a way that is congruent to what it has already been for a long time internally— but now other people can see it. I can attest to this, as I'm finally where I wanted to be. It was a long process, both mentally and physically, and did take a while for it to really sink in that I was now a woman and have succeeded in transitioning outwardly.

However, the medical journey continues. As my primary care physician, internist Dr. Kathy Renschler, told me, transgender healthcare is just one part of a total patient's care, like treatment for diabetes or asthma. I have to continue taking care of myself, keeping my appointments with my doctors, exercising, taking my hormones and performing the routine of dilation. I kept my primary care physician because all along she was sensitive to the issues that went with taking care of me, both before and after my transition, and she wants me to live a healthy life as the person I want to be.

CHAPTER 3

UNDERSTANDING YOUR LEGAL FOUNDATION

Despite cultural and policy fluctuations from one presidential administration to the next, there is a well-founded set of legal precedents that protect transgender individuals in the US and around the world. For instance, the Trump administration's 2017 attempt to ban transgender men and women from the military has been stayed because federal judges have determined that the practice is discriminatory. Beyond the courtroom, the pushback by the LGBTQ+ community and its allies against overt acts of discrimination emanating from the administration or outside the federal government show that there is a pervasive societal awareness and acceptance of the benefits of having a diverse and protected population.

Yet many of the transgender individuals, as well as the legal experts I've interviewed for this book, feel that an underlying transgender bias remains, which may affect transgender rights in the future. If the political leadership indicates that we should not be a diverse and inclusive society, then it is setting a tone where discrimination and improper treatment of any outsider is acceptable, and that includes people in the LGBTQ+ community. This belief is just one of the many factors people take into account as they weigh their options for making a transition. However, consistent progress is being made, and even though some legislative and judicial decisions might not be ideal, the transgender community is growing, enlisting more allies, and employing effective tactics to enable adoption of LGBTQ+-friendly policies, and highlighting issues that threaten the community. As you are considering a transition, if you are concerned about your current political environment, know that the community will support you. Collectively, we will continue to fight to improve and spread a culture of diversity and inclusion, especially in the workplace.

Labor and employment attorney Denise Visconti, who is the Office Managing Shareholder with Littler Mendelson P.C., in San Diego, California, has seen a definite shift with employers creating a more positive, diverse, and open work environment. She is starting to see companies being proactive and developing and implementing gender transition policies. In the more than 15 years she has been practicing, the number of companies contacting her regarding employee transitions is steadily increasing, from once a month ten years ago to at least two to three times a week at present. She told me, "The number of people who are transitioning or at least alerting their company to an intention to transition has certainly increased. While some who transition then seek new employment, they are at least beginning their transition while still employed."

Denise believes that companies that have proactively engaged transitioning employees are looking to make the transition go smoothly, with the goal of the employee staying on after the transition. However, there are many more companies, both large and small, that have not yet had to accommodate transgender employees. The purpose of this chapter is for you to understand your rights. Some of the prevailing laws have been enacted at the state or even local levels, while others are enforced at the federal level. When it comes to the workplace, there are two main areas of the law transitioning individuals need to become familiar with: general civil rights and anti-discrimination laws. These areas then influence employment law for private sector employees (federal contractors and sub-contractors are covered by a separate, explicit prohibition on transgender or sexual orientation discrimination in employment) and the prevailing climate regarding terminations or unfair employment practices.

Understanding Title VII: the federally mandated guidelines

The Equal Employment Opportunity Commission (EEOC) is responsible for enforcing federal laws that make it illegal to discriminate against a job applicant or an employee. When it comes to transgender discrimination, the EEOC is concerned with Title VII of the Civil Rights Act of 1964. This law makes it illegal to discriminate against someone on the basis of race, color, religion, national origin, or sex, which is currently understood to include pregnancy, gender identity, and sexual orientation. The law also makes it illegal to retaliate against a person who has complained about discrimination, filed a charge of discrimination, or participated in an employment discrimination investigation or lawsuit. Most employers (with at least 15 employees), labor unions, and employment agencies are covered under Title VII. Employment practices, including job advertisements, recruitment, hiring, job referrals, assignments and promotions, pay and benefits, and discipline and discharge, are all covered under this Act.

Title VII does not explicitly include sexual orientation or gender identity in its list of protections. However, the Commission interprets the statute's sex discrimination provision as prohibiting discrimination against employees on the basis of sexual orientation and gender identity. This is based upon US Supreme Court case law and other court decisions which hold that employment actions motivated by gender stereotyping are unlawful sex discrimination. The language on the EEOC's website is clear:

> Discrimination against an individual because of gender identity, including transgender status, or because of sexual orientation is discrimination because of sex in violation of Title VII... Through investigation, conciliation, and litigation of charges by individuals against private sector employers, as well as hearings and appeals for federal sector workers, the Commission has taken the position that existing sex discrimination provisions in Title VII protect lesbian, gay, bisexual, and transgender (LGBT) applicants and employees against employment bias.

The EEOC is actively enforcing Title VII through its Washington DC office and 53 satellite offices across the country. One of its goals is to protect transgender individuals and to prohibit discrimination in the workplace, and to go after employers who fail either to act appropriately or to get their employees to act appropriately toward transgender individuals. These protections apply regardless of any contrary state or local laws. As a result of the EEOC's efforts, it has raised the profile of transgender employees in the workplace and increased compliance. What's more, a growing number of court decisions have endorsed the Commission's interpretation of Title VII.

WHAT DOES UNLAWFUL SEX DISCRIMINATION LOOK LIKE?

Some examples of transgender-related claims that the EEOC views as unlawful sex discrimination include:

- Failing to hire an applicant because she/he is transgender.

- Firing an employee because she/he is planning on or has made a gender transition.

- Denying an employee equal access to a common restroom corresponding with the employee's gender identity.

- Harassing an employee because of a gender transition, such as by intentionally and persistently failing to use the name and gender pronoun that corresponds to the gender identity with which the employee identifies, and which the employee has communicated to management and other employees.

For more information on Title VII and how it applies to LGBT+ employees, visit: www.eeoc.gov/eeoc/newsroom/wysk/enforce ment_protections_lgbt_workers.cfm

Your legal rights: state by state

Your legal rights in the workplace are dependent on the state in which you live. Some states offer more protection than Title VII, while many others are less friendly to the LGBTQ+ community. However, federal law does not prevent the states from having more comprehensive protection against discrimination and harassment than federal law provides. For instance, if you are a trans person and being discriminated against or harassed at work because of that fact, the best remedy could be to sue for discrimination in your state. If a state or local law permits or does not prohibit discrimination based on sexual orientation or gender identity, the EEOC will still enforce Title VII's discrimination prohibitions against covered employers in that jurisdiction.

The majority of US states do not have laws and policies in place that support or protect transitioning employees. The Human Rights Campaign (HRC) is America's largest civil rights organization working to achieve lesbian, gay, bisexual, transgender, and queer equality. One of the many areas it monitors is discrimination against members of the LGBTQ+ community. It is important to stay abreast of LGBTQ+ legislation on the state level. This can vary significantly, and a good resource to track what's going on across the US is the State Equality Index, compiled by the HRC.[1]

In its 2018 assessment, the HRC found that only 20 states and the District of Columbia legally protect employees from discrimination based on both sexual orientation and gender identity. They include:

- California
- Colorado
- Connecticut
- Delaware
- District of Columbia
- Hawaii
- Illinois
- Iowa
- Maine
- Maryland
- Massachusetts
- Minnesota
- Nevada
- New Jersey
- New Mexico
- New York
- Oregon
- Rhode Island
- Utah
- Vermont
- Washington

Another six states prohibit discrimination only against *public (government) employees* based on sexual orientation and gender identity. These include:

- Indiana
- Kentucky
- Michigan
- Montana
- Pennsylvania
- Virginia

---

1   https://assets2.hrc.org/files/assets/resources/SEI-2017-Report-FINAL.pdf.

State regulations regarding health insurance

According to the HRC, many states have regulated health insurance policy options as they relate to transgender healthcare.

States with bans on insurance exclusions for transgender healthcare:

- California
- Colorado
- Connecticut
- Delaware
- District of Columbia
- Hawaii
- Maryland
- Massachusetts
- Minnesota
- Nevada
- New York
- Oregon
- Pennsylvania
- Rhode Island
- Vermont
- Washington

States with transgender-inclusive health benefits for state employees:

- California
- Connecticut
- District of Columbia
- Maryland
- Massachusetts
- Minnesota
- Nevada
- New York
- Oregon
- Rhode Island
- Vermont
- Washington

States with transgender coverage *exclusions* in Medicaid:

- Alaska
- Arizona
- Georgia
- Hawaii
- Idaho
- Iowa

- Maine
- Michigan
- Missouri
- Nebraska
- Nevada
- New Hampshire

- New Jersey
- Tennessee
- Texas
- West Virginia
- Wisconsin
- Wyoming

State ratings for policies on equality and gender identity

A 2017 report published by the Movement Advancement Project[2] and supported by the National Center for Transgender Equality rates all 50 states and the District of Columbia regarding existing transgender policies. Those states with equality policies that are rated highly have clear protections from bullying and discrimination in schools, access to medically necessary healthcare, and offer clear and accessible ways for a trans person to change their name and gender on identification. They also offer protection from being unfairly fired, evicted, or refused access to public spaces. As you can imagine, states that are categorized in the "medium" and "low" ratings offer fewer protections and on a diminishing scale, and the states with negative ratings for equality policies do not offer any. Over half of LGBT+ people live in states with negative or low gender identity policy ratings. While it might not be possible to relocate to a friendlier state, it might be worth considering.

---

2   The Movement Advancement Project (MAP) is an independent think tank that provides rigorous research, insight, and analysis that help speed equality for LGBT people. MAP works collaboratively with LGBT organizations, advocates and funders, providing information, analysis, and resources that help coordinate and strengthen efforts for maximum impact. MAP's policy research informs the public and policymakers about the legal and policy needs of LGBT people and their families. www.lgbtmap.org/equality-maps.

States with high ratings for equality and gender identity policies:

- California
- Colorado
- Connecticut
- District of Columbia
- Illinois
- Maryland
- Massachusetts
- Minnesota
- New York
- Oregon
- Rhode Island
- Vermont
- Washington

States with medium ratings for equality and gender identity policies:

- Delaware
- Hawaii
- Maine
- New Jersey
- New Mexico
- Nevada
- Pennsylvania

States with low ratings for equality and gender identity policies:

- Alaska
- Florida
- Indiana
- Iowa
- Michigan
- New Hampshire
- Utah
- Virginia

States with negative ratings for equality and gender identity policies:

- Alabama
- Arizona
- Arkansas
- Georgia
- Idaho
- Kansas
- Kentucky
- Louisiana

- Mississippi
- Missouri
- Montana
- Nebraska
- North Carolina
- North Dakota
- Ohio
- Oklahoma
- South Carolina
- South Dakota
- Tennessee
- Texas
- West Virginia
- Wisconsin
- Wyoming

The highest rated states will afford the most protection across a wide range of issues, although the range within these groups also varies. For instance, a new requirement in California from the Fair Employment and Housing Act mandates that employers in California educate all managers on transgender issues, in addition to educating them on workplace harassment. This requirement is not shared in other high-equality states. The same 20 states that the HRC designated as transgender-employee friendly, with the exception of Utah, also prohibit discrimination for public accommodations (bathrooms) based on sexual orientation and gender identity.

The community in which you live within a high-equality state may also matter. Bigger cities, which may be more diverse and progressive, can ensure more protections (generally called ordinances) than more rural and conservative regions. For instance, New York City, Philadelphia, San Francisco, Boston, and Chicago all extended anti-discrimination protections to include gender identity and gender expression as far back as 2002. What's more, these regulations have paved the way for larger gains on gender discrimination issues, and may help turn the tide within their state. For example, Dallas (which is in a "low" protection state), provides by municipal ordinance for gender (including gender identity) protections in employment, notwithstanding the fact that far less protection exists at the Texas state level. The precedents set by these major cities have affected policies in many other US cities, with 64 cities providing trans protections by the fall of 2005. According to the HRC, as of January 2017, at least 225 cities and counties prohibit employment discrimination on the basis of gender identity in employment ordinances that govern public and private employers.

The first legal precedent: *Macy v. Holder*

In 2012, the Equal Employment Opportunity Commission ruled on a case and established a legal precedent for transgender rights in the workplace. It held that the "intentional discrimination against a transgender individual because that person is transgender is, by definition, discrimination 'based on...sex,' and such discrimination therefore violates Title VII."

In 2010, Mia Macy, a transgender woman, was a police detective in Phoenix, Arizona, who decided to relocate to San Francisco. According to her formal complaint, Mia was still known as a male at that time. Her supervisor in Phoenix told her that the Bureau of Alcohol, Tobacco, Firearms and Explosives had a position open at its Walnut Creek, California, crime laboratory for which she was qualified. She discussed the position with the Director of the Walnut Creek laboratory by telephone, while still presenting as a man. Following the conversation, the Director told her she would be able to have the position assuming no problems arose during her background check. The Director also told her that she would be contacted by an outside firm named Aspen of DC to begin the necessary paperwork.

On March 29, 2011, Mia informed Aspen via email that she was in the process of transitioning from male to female and she requested that Aspen inform the Director of the Walnut Creek laboratory of this change. On April 8, 2011, she received an email from Aspen's Director of Operations stating that, due to federal budget reductions, the position at Walnut Creek was no longer available. Mia believed she was informed that the position had been cut because the Agency did not want to hire her due to the fact she was transgender. She then filed a claim with the EEOC, and her case became the first time that the EEOC held that Title VII covered transgender individuals.

The EEOC's April 20, 2012 decision to side with Mia Macy has largely informed how private employers are expected to treat transgender workers under federal law. However, the legal impact of Macy is incomplete. Because Macy is a decision by the EEOC, the Commission will take seriously complaints of gender identity discrimination and will work with victims to remedy that discrimination. In cases involving the federal government, the EEOC has authority to adjudicate discrimination claims and issue legally binding decisions. This means that federal employees can fairly say that they are now protected provided that they elect to have their claims adjudicated by the EEOC instead of a federal court. But the EEOC's power over private employers is much more limited. Although the EEOC has the authority to investigate complaints against a private employer and to assist the parties in reaching a mutually agreeable resolution, it has no power to force a private employer to treat an employee differently or to agree that transgender people are protected. If an employer insists on continuing a discriminatory practice, then the EEOC can sue for damages on behalf of the employee or the employee can sue the employer and could then invoke the *Macy v. Holder* ruling. However, *Macy v. Holder* only specifically applied to federal employees so whether it would be considered a precedent for other workplaces is unclear.

BEST PRACTICES FOR WORKPLACE RIGHTS

Your rights in the workplace can go far beyond the issues outlined by the EEOC. According to the Transgender Law Center, the following rights are best practices in the workplace in terms of creating an environment that is friendly to transitioning and transgender employees:

- The right to use the restroom of the gender you identify with.

- The right to be called by your preferred name, even before a legal name change.

- The right to be addressed by your preferred pronoun.

- The right to dress in a manner consistent with your gender expression.

- The right to be treated with dignity during the transition.

- The right to medical privacy and the ability to take medical leave.

Understanding international laws that affect transgender workers

According to the HRC website, some countries do provide legal protections for transgender people. In the European Union (EU), a 1996 decision of the European Court of Justice in *P v. S and Cornwall County Council* provided protections from employment discrimination related to "gender reassignment." The UK formalized this EU decision when it passed the 1999 Sex Discrimination (Gender Reassignment) Regulations. This law provides protections for transgender people "intend[ing] to undergo...undergoing or hav[ing] undergone gender reassignment," and applies to any stage of employment. The European Court of Human Rights has continued to uphold and require protections for transgender people, and both the UK and Spain also have laws that allow transgender people to change their name and gender on official documents without needing to undergo surgery.

Outside Europe, South Africa and many states and territories of Australia also prohibit discrimination against transgender people. Businesses that operate in these countries are prohibited from discriminating against or harassing transgender employees. Companies in the US and abroad can also extend protections for transgender employees to their global operations.

Just as in the US, there are transgender support services around the globe. A directed web search for any given country will be helpful to identify local resources.

What is a "bathroom bill"?

A bathroom bill is the common name for legislation or a statute that defines access to public facilities—specifically restrooms—for transgender individuals. Bathroom bills affect access to sex-segregated public facilities based on a determination of someone's sex as defined by their sex at birth, their sex as listed on their birth certificate, or the sex that corresponds to their gender identity. A bathroom bill can either be inclusive or exclusive of transgender individuals.

Legislation in many states has been adopted since the landmark 2013 case, in which the Colorado Civil Rights Division ruled in favor of allowing a transgender student to use the girls' bathroom at her elementary school. It was the first ruling of its kind in the US and one of the first high-profile transgender rights cases. Since then, public opinion regarding transgender bathroom rights has been mixed. A Pew Research poll[3] from October 2016 found that about half of US adults (51%) stated that transgender individuals should be "allowed to use public restrooms that correspond with the gender they currently identify with," with nearly as many (46%) taking the opposite position—"transgender people should be required to use bathrooms that match the gender they were born into." Critics of

---

3   Lipka, M. (2016) *Americans are divided over which public bathrooms transgender people should use.* Pew Research Center, October, 2016. Available at www.pewresearch. org/fact-tank/2016/10/03/americans-are-divided-over-which-public-bathrooms-transgender-people-should-use.

bills that exclude transgender individuals from restrooms that conform to their gender identity argue that they do not make public restrooms any safer for cisgender (non-transgender) people, and that they make public restrooms less safe for both transgender people and gender non-conforming people. Proponents of excluding legislation believe it is necessary to maintain privacy, protect what they claim to be an innate sense of modesty, prevent voyeurism, assault, molestation, and rape, and retain psychological comfort.

As there is ongoing legislation around this issue in various US states, the most progressive companies are setting their own policies that support transgender employees. For example, the following language is included in the Dow Chemical workplace transition guidelines:

> Employees shall have equal access to all workplace restrooms and other facilities corresponding to their gender identity. All employees have a right to safe and appropriate restroom facilities, including the right to use a restroom that corresponds to the employee's gender identity, regardless of the employee's sex assigned at birth. For example, transgender women are permitted to use the women's restroom, and transgender men are permitted to use the men's restroom; the decision of which restroom is the most appropriate and safest to use should be left to the employee. Some employees—transgender or non-transgender—may desire additional privacy. Where possible, site management can make available a unisex single-stall restroom that can be used by any employee who has a need for increased privacy, regardless of the reason.

The legal landscape evolves slowly

The shifting politics of presidential administrations is particularly troubling for the LGBTQ+ community. While administrations come and go, their legacies live on through the federal judges that are appointed to circuit courts, appeals courts, and the US

Supreme Court. When a president selects extremists for the federal judiciary who demonstrate contempt for whole segments of the population, it undermines the essential impartiality of our courts. As any case proceeds through the court system, unenlightened judges could reverse rulings or reinterpret opinions that might dramatically change our protections in the workplace.

Attorney Denise Visconti explained the following to me, "I think we are in some challenging times for the community. The problem is that the anti-LGBTQ sentiment that is emanating from the [Trump] administration has the potential to outlast his presidency for many decades. First, his rhetoric signals the country that it is okay to express an anti-LGBTQ sentiment. But in terms of the legal system, his judicial appointments set the stage for a lasting change in protections. Let's say someone lives in a state like Indiana or Texas that does not have a state law prohibiting transgender discrimination. If that person announces their intention to transition and is promptly fired they can then file a lawsuit. Or even if it is not so overt, and instead of being fired they are slowly performance-managed out of their position and they then file a lawsuit believing that it was based on their gender identity or their announcement to transition. That lawsuit gets into federal court and a federal judge finds there is not much, if any, precedent in their circuit which covers that state, and decides that Title VII does not cover someone who is transgender. That person then appeals the decision, and until the case works its way up to the Supreme Court, years can go by. By this time, if another liberal Supreme Court justice retires and there is a conservative appointment, the Supreme Court could issue a majority conservative decision on whether Title VII covers transgender individuals. Once the Supreme Court issues a ruling, that does become the law and it takes a lot of effort to reverse it."

This is why it is so important to be aware of the federal judges being appointed in your state, and to become active in local politics. Judicial activism is one of the best ways to ensure that judges uphold LGBTQ+ rights and reflect a tolerant and diverse mindset.

Recently, the LGBTQ+ community has had some success in preventing the confirmation of discriminatory and intolerant judges. According to an article written by Julianna S. Gonen in *The Hill*, one-third of Trump's judicial nominees have a record of open hostility to the rights of LGBT Americans.[4] Yet in contrast, a recent opinion halting Trump's transgender military ban shows how sitting judge Colleen Kollar-Kotelly, of the United States District Court for the District of Columbia, who was originally appointed to the federal judiciary by Ronald Reagan but was appointed to her current seat by Bill Clinton, described the transgender community, "The Court is aware of no argument or evidence suggesting that being transgender in any way limits one's ability to contribute to society. The exemplary military service of Plaintiffs in this case certainly suggests that it does not. ... Many have years of experience in the military. Some have decades. They have been deployed on active duty in Iraq and Afghanistan. They have and continue to serve with distinction."[5]

This is one example of the balance of power between the judicial branch and the executive branch of our government. But it also points directly to how the impact of a single election cycle can last far into the future. Knowing your rights is the first step but advocating for them in the ballot box is equally important.

In addition to the effect a new administration can have on the judicial branch, it can also change long-held policies and guidelines implemented by the government. For instance, in January 2018, the US Department of Health and Human Services announced the creation of a new department, named the Division of Conscience and Religious Freedom, whose mandate is to "protect" doctors, nurses and other healthcare workers who refuse to take part in

---

4   http://thehill.com/blogs/congress-blog/judicial/367445-time-for-a-reset-on-judicial-nominations.

5   *Jane Doe 1 et al. v. Donald Trump et al.* [2017] Civil Action No. 17–1597 (CKK), p.61. Available at https://ecf.dcd.uscourts.gov/cgi-bin/show_public_doc?2017cv1597-61.

procedures like abortion, and to give them the ability to exclude providing care to patients based on the provider's moral and religious convictions. The establishment of this department opens the door to reversing an Obama-era policy that barred healthcare workers from refusing to treat transgender individuals or people who have had or are seeking abortions.

One can only imagine that those conscience objections could expand to allow healthcare workers to refuse services to gay, lesbian, and transgender people. Whether this may affect your ability to access healthcare where you live remains to be seen, but it is a troubling sign and another reason to stay abreast of policy issues and support the American Civil Liberties Union (ACLU) and National Center for Transgender Equality (NCTE), who are working to enable and improve access to healthcare for the LGBTQ+ community.

My brush with workplace discrimination

Before my "nail polish and earrings" confrontation with the HR department, I had already consulted with an attorney, and I knew that transgender individuals are protected against workplace discrimination by law in California. During that first uncomfortable HR talk, I became instantly aware that how I was going to be treated in the office would change once I decided to announce my intention to transition.

The HR employee made it clear that because she was unaware of my transgender status, I was not considered a member of a "protected class." This meant that they could fire me without cause if I continued to slowly explore a change in outward gender expression without declaring my intention to transition. In that moment, I knew I had just two options: I could declare myself as transgender, even though I wasn't personally ready to announce my transition; or I could accept HR's advice to remove the nail polish and earrings, which would effectively force me back into the closet until I was ready to come out at the time of my own choosing.

My immediate self-preservation instinct was to limit the short-term damage until I could process the situation, so I agreed to take out the earrings and get the polish removed for the time being, and thereby toe the company line. My reaction was influenced by my deep commitment to the company—I believed in the company's mission and values, so when HR made suggestions for how I should present myself, I believed that they had good intentions. Instinctively, I believed at first that they were just trying to make me conform to what they thought was the proper presentation for a white, male vice president. And, like all victims of harassment or abuse, I second-guessed my own motives. Maybe my attire *was* inappropriate; maybe this awkward conversation *was* my fault. I also began to worry that if this was how they treated a white male at my executive level, what would they think of me once I was a transgender female?

I immediately called my girlfriend (now my wife), Stella. Besides her, I had no other place to turn at such short notice. There were no colleagues in whom I had confided. There were no other transgender employees, to my knowledge. And having lived for over 50 years as a straight white male, it didn't even occur to me to call a legal helpline or the ACLU. As I look back, my blindness to what was actually going on probably reflected the fact that I had never been discriminated against; I had always been protected by my white male privilege.

Stella suggested that I contact my attorney, who was very surprised that HR had directly confronted me about my gender expression, which is illegal according to California law. After discussions with my attorney, I understood that HR was correct in that until I stated my intention to transition I was not necessarily part of a protected class. Once I understood the pros and cons of my various courses of action, I decided to immediately declare myself as a transgender employee and disclose my intention to transition at work. Armed with my attorney's input, I began to create a paper trail of documents regarding my transition, making notes of my conversations with HR and company executives. My attorney assisted me in preparing for likely interactions in various workplace contexts. The goal was to make it difficult for the employer to discriminate against me and, if it did, to make it more likely that I would prevail if litigation were required.

In retrospect, the best decision I made leading up to that day was that I had already understood my legal rights in advance (an initial consultation for when I decided to announce my transition). Had I been completely blindsided when HR came to talk to me, I would have had to research my rights that tumultuous day, which would have made me even more confused and worried about my career. But because I was prepared and knew that I lived in a state where I couldn't be fired after I made the announcement that I was planning to transition, I was able to make the decision to move forward toward my true self with both eyes open and with a good understanding of the legal landscape.

Legal requirements for a name and gender transition: paperwork and documentation

Many states will allow you to formally change your gender on legal documents after you transition. Every state, and even every county within each state, may have different requirements and policies. According to attorney Denise Visconti, there are legal requirements relating to social security numbers and payroll documents, which cannot be changed to an individual's chosen or preferred name prior to a legal name and gender marker change.

There are federal documents you need to change as well. Your passport is a federal document, and you need to make sure that it is current and accurately reflects your legal identity and gender expression. Your Social Security number will stay the same, but you will want your identification card to reflect your new name.

According to the HRC, the states with laws and policies that facilitate gender marker change on drivers' licenses and birth certificates include:

- Arizona
- California
- District of Columbia
- Hawaii

- Illinois
- Oregon
- Maryland
- Pennsylvania
- Minnesota
- Rhode Island
- Nevada
- Washington
- New York

The states with laws and policies that facilitate gender marker change on drivers' licenses only include:

- Alaska
- Michigan
- Colorado
- Missouri
- Connecticut
- New Hampshire
- Delaware
- New Jersey
- Idaho
- North Dakota
- Indiana
- New Mexico
- Iowa
- Ohio
- Kansas
- Vermont
- Maine
- Virginia
- Massachusetts
- West Virginia

Unfortunately, there are states with laws and policies that *prevent* transgender people from receiving appropriate identification. These include:

- Idaho
- Tennessee
- Ohio

I started my paper transition when I applied to change my name and gender with the state of California, which requires a court decree. This process is administered at the county level and can take months to navigate, including posting a public notification of the name change in a local paper, in case I had outstanding debts or other nefarious reasons to legally change my name. It took two or three months just to get an appointment at the San Mateo County offices to change my name and gender. From the time I started my application, it was probably four months until I had my official court hearing. The ability to get an official court decree alone is one of the many benefits of living and working in California.

While I was waiting for my court date, but after I changed my gender expression, I had to travel to London for business. I already had transitioned at work and was dressing as a woman all of the time. While I had not yet legally changed my name or gender, if I wanted to go on the trip I would have to use my existing "David Pizzuti" passport. I was worried that I wasn't going to be allowed into the UK with a passport which did not match my gender expression, but I thought it was worth a try because I wanted as many people on my international team to see the new me. My therapist suggested that I use that passport and she would write a letter for me which stated who I was legally and that my gender dysphoria required that I present at all times a woman, and that this had worked for her other clients who had traveled internationally.

I had no trouble getting on the plane in San Francisco, but when I landed in London things got interesting. When I got to passport control, the agent took a very long moment looking at my passport, and my face. He then asked me, "Did you bring the right passport?" In a soft voice, I answered that yes, that was my passport but that I was transgender and was starting my transition. I couldn't really blame the clerk since I looked like an old gray-haired man in the photo, so I pulled out the letter from my therapist, and explained the situation. The agent looked at me quizzically and then said he needed to ask his supervisor to come over and provide some guidance. The supervisor pleasantly listened to my situation, looked at the passport and my therapist's letter, looked back at me again, and then asked the clerk, "Did anything come up?" This question was in reference to the agent's scan of my passport against the international database of known criminals. When the agent said that I wasn't a risk, his supervisor smiled at me, and I was let in.

After that incident, and until I had my legal name and identity documents changed, I always carried the therapist's letter with me. Even now that I have legally changed my name and gender on state and federal identity documents, I still carry my court decree everywhere I go. It proves that Dana and David are the same person. I have had to show it more than a few times over the last few years.

As soon as you get a court decree, you can start changing your other legal documents. With my court decree in hand, freshly certified by the judge and the clerk, I went to the social security office and got a temporary social security card, and then to the Department of Motor Vehicles for a new driver's license with a new picture. The National Center for Transgender Equality website (https://transequality.org/documents) has the best resources for how to change your identification, and it suggests other legal documents to consider changing (remember, the ease at which you can make these changes varies state by state):

- Bank accounts

- Birth certificate

- Immigration documents

- Insurance policies

- Military/veteran records

- Mortgages, title insurance policies, and the deeds to your home

- Passport

- Selective Service records

- Will

- Advanced directive

There will be other documents that can be changed once these are altered. For instance, I'm still finding that I'm changing my frequent flyer accounts, which require a copy of my driver's license. Using the court decree, I had my college and medical school alma maters reissue my diplomas with my new name and gender. I also was able to change my medical licenses, medical board accreditation, credit cards, insurance, and medical records.

In the workplace, you should work with your HR department to update your personal records. These include company directories and photos, name plates or name tags, email addresses, business cards, archived performance reviews, personnel files and other employee records, benefits documents, and other internal documents.

Expect the best, plan for the worst: charting a course of legal action

As with anything, knowledge is power. Once you fully understand your legal standing, and what your state affords you in terms of protecting you from discrimination, you can assume that every aspect of your transition in the workplace will go smoothly. Companies both large and small want to retain good employees, and, more importantly, don't want to engage in lawsuits. However, while the protections we've discussed in this chapter are clear, and attorney Denise Visconti sees an upward trend in employees transitioning successfully, she also sees an upward trend in the number of charges being filed against employers by transgender workers.

Discrimination comes in many different guises. Overt discrimination would involve being fired soon after a transition or right after you announce that you're planning on transitioning. A subtler, more challenging, and more difficult to prove discrimination occurs when you announce your intention to transition, and then weeks later you are passed over for a promotion or put on a performance improvement plan, when the only thing that has changed has been your announcement.

If you feel that you are being discriminated against, follow my lead—consult competent legal counsel before trying to handle the situation yourself within the company. Get advice as to how to proceed before going to the HR department or the boss. Avoid pitfalls. Know your rights.

Major companies have built internal safeguards within their HR departments. Often, a company has an internal complaints process, and many have "diversity and inclusion" groups, whose job is to make sure the company is not harassing or discriminating against people, to be responsible for training the workforce around harassment and discrimination issues, and to act as an available sounding board when there are issues regarding the workplace environment.

Once you have obtained legal guidance privately, the first step is to bring your complaint to the HR department or the most senior manager on your team. According to the Transgender Law Center, starting here will give your employer a chance to stop the discrimination before it becomes worse. It also creates a record that you tried to resolve the situation before seeking legal action.

Some companies also have hotlines that are managed by third parties which are meant to be impartial and potentially anonymous resources for employees who would like to report harassment or discrimination, which they either experience first-hand or witness happening to others. Remember, according the EEOC, you cannot be retaliated against—fired, demoted, or treated unfairly—simply for bringing up an issue of possible discrimination or harassment in good faith. Even if your claim is not substantiated or does not qualify as harassment or discrimination, you are protected against retaliation so long as you were reasonable in bringing the situation to the attention of your employer. According to employment attorney Rick Levine, of Levine & Baker in San Francisco, more cases are won by employees because they experienced retaliation compared to actual discrimination; while they may not be able to prove at trial that they were really discriminated against, they can prove that raising the issue resulted in retaliation.

If your internal complaint is not taken seriously, and the situation is not properly remedied, the next step is to go outside the company to lodge a complaint. There are numerous options to explore, such as filing a complaint with your state fair employment agency or with the EEOC, or retaining outside legal services, but choosing which one to follow might be dependent on your financial resources. There are many places an individual can go for free legal advice and support, such as state agencies, which will make complaints against employers. For example, California has the Department of Fair Employment and Housing, which has as its mission to protect employees in California from unlawful discrimination in employment. If your state doesn't have a specific law that protects against discrimination based on gender identity and expression, then a local EEOC office, found in most major cities, can help. There are also not-for-profit organisations, like Lambda Legal, which assist LGBTQ+ individuals in filing a charge, or can direct you to an agency that can help, or potentially represent you. You may also be able to take your complaint to your local human rights agency, which at the very least can offer you guidance. You may also be able to find help through national organizations like the ACLU, which has a specific area on its website dedicated to transgender rights, including a form for submitting a request for help (https://action.aclu.org/secure/report-LGBThiv-discrimination).

Transgender-friendly law clinics, as well as individual attorneys who specialize in representing transgender clients, can be found in most major cities; for example, the Transgender Law Center started in Oakland, California, and is now one of the biggest national resources on legal issues facing the trans community. It does not take on individual cases; instead, it focuses on high-profile discrimination cases such as the so-called "Bathroom Bill" in North Carolina, and policy issues. GLBTQ Legal Advocates & Defenders (GLAD) is a national organization based in Boston, Massachusetts. Its mission is to prevent discrimination through strategic litigation, public policy advocacy, and education. It offers legal services, including translation, which is available in over 200 languages.

The National Center for Transgender Equality is located in Washington and focuses on maintaining transgender rights, including access to health insurance. According to Mara Keisling, the Executive Director of NCTE, the support it offers to trans people is primarily around policy initiatives and self-advocacy. NCTE created the Trans Legal Services Network to ensure that every transgender person has access to legal representation for issues they may face. The Network brings together over 60 organizations to share advice, technical support, and legal resources. Its Trans Legal Services Advisory Council is made up of law firms dedicated to providing legal support for the Network.

Another option is private legal counsel. Private attorneys (that is, not GLAD or other public interest attorneys who offer counsel for free) generally charge by the hour or by the consultation unless they believe you have a good claim against the defendant that would produce money from which they could take a percentage as a fee if you prevailed (a "contingent fee"). Unless you have already been fired or otherwise suffered financial damages as result of the employer's discrimination, you are likely to have to pay hourly, but that needn't be a great deal of money. It might only take a couple of hours of your time, and your attorney's time.

Your local bar association can help you find employment lawyers. If you have a relationship with any attorney, ask them for a referral: if they don't specialize in this area of the law, they may know other lawyers who do. Depending on where you live, you might also need to have an attorney help you process your legal documents surrounding your transition.

People are frequently reluctant to seek private legal counsel because they think a lawyer will push them to do something they don't want to do, such as bring a case to trial. However, most lawyers operate as advisors who work for the best interest of their clients. They are looking to resolve their client's problems in a way that is best for the client at a reasonable cost. According to Rick Levine, most employment attorneys who focus their practices on representing employees, rather than employers, are committed to being resources for the less economically powerful party in disputes (or potential disputes) between employees and employers. He suggests that employees should think of such employment lawyers as a resource not to fear. Such attorneys will both have the experience to provide the counsel you need and to do so efficiently.

Final considerations

You now have reviewed the necessary groundwork for a successful transition. Knowing who is on your support team, understanding your medical choices, and knowing your legal protections are critical to helping you decide if you are ready for a transition. The rest of the book assumes that you are ready to make an announcement at work. Even if you are still undecided, read on, so that you can learn from my experience and see what happens once you are ready. The following two questions are meant to help you determine your work options and availability for ongoing support:

- Do you think your co-workers, from the boss to peers to subordinates, will continue to respect you after you transition, and would you be able to continue to work together? The remainder of the book will help you sort through office politics and culture so that you can not only survive but thrive in your workplace.

- How would you feel about transitioning and remaining in the same work environment, or would you prefer to change jobs or transfer after your transition to make a fresh start? If you've realized that you might be better off with a fresh start, Chapter 10 may prove especially enlightening.

Since my announcement in 2015 I've never looked back, and although my work experience did not turn out to be exactly what I expected, my career trajectory has been better than I could have imagined. I can say that I feel totally supported by my current employer, and I go to work each day happy that I transitioned. I have also been heartened by the support of and solidarity with the transgender community and our allies, particularly the LGBTQ+ community. Collectively, we are working to further the ideals of living authentically and being able to express your true self to make it easier for anyone to transition successfully.

PART II

BRINGING YOUR TRANSITION TO WORK

CHAPTER 4

MAKING YOUR INITIAL DECLARATION

When you believe the time is right, you will tell your employer that you intend to transition. The goal of this chapter is to provide a best practice approach for this declaration. Remember, you are not asking for permission. At the same time, you will need to work with your employer so that you can manage your transition, including the medical aspects, so that it does not disrupt the business or sideline your career plans.

Your declaration and the reaction to your new gender expression may be received differently depending on whether you are transitioning from male to female or female to male. I have found that transgender males sometimes have an easier time, because many have adopted a more neutral or androgynous gender expression well before they announce their intention to transition. For instance, before Morgan transitioned from female to male in a small office environment of just 12 employees, he had always worn his hair short, and never wore dresses or skirts to work, opting for wearing pants and a dress shirt and a tie. He also opted to keep his birth name, Morgan, which can be used for both genders.

However, when a traditionally gendered man seems to "suddenly" decide to express his gender as a woman it's a more obvious change. This is why it is particularly important for those undergoing MTF transition to plan the announcement carefully in advance and understand that even the slightest changes in gender expression may still be noted by co-workers and management. For instance, before I declared myself as trans, my dysphoria at expressing myself as male at work and then as female outside work was becoming more pronounced. As I mentioned previously, I decided to test the waters toward a more feminine gender expression by getting my ears pierced and wearing clear nail polish on short nails. Even though I worked in the San Francisco Bay Area, where many men pierced both ears, I was surprised that management had noted my change in appearance and actually decided to send an emissary from HR to confront me about it. Because of this one confrontation, I lost control over the timing of my declaration. In retrospect, despite my long tenure at the company, I underestimated how conservative and restrictive the corporate culture would be. If I had known that then, I might not have made any outward changes until I was completely ready to declare my transition.

Before you declare: the workplace assessment checklist

How well your employer will react to your declaration may directly correspond with how they deal with diversity and inclusion in general. Because of the EEOC ruling, even the most conservative companies, and their management, have to "tolerate" your transition, but they don't have to be empathetic, or celebrate it as more progressive companies will. As IBM's Connie Rice stated at the 2017 Transform Tech Summit, "There's inclusion policies, and there's actual inclusion."

It's perfectly normal to worry about how your transition is going to be perceived, even once you know that you cannot lose your job solely due to your transition. Knowing your company culture and where you stand within the organization will help you allay these fears and prepare your transition announcement. Answer the following questions to see where your company currently stands regarding transgender policies.

1. Your work status

    a. Where are you in the corporate hierarchy? Who is your boss, and can you tell them directly before going to HR, or afterwards?

    b. Are you part of a large team? Do you have direct interface with customers? Are you ready for a full disclosure, including everyone you work with?

    c. What are the demographics of senior management and co-workers?

    d. What has been your recent performance history? This question is important since it is a reflection of how you may be perceived by management and the value you bring to the organization. If you have had negative performance reviews, it may affect the prism through which your management views your ability to carry out your job responsibilities. It should not matter but it is unfortunate that some managers may not be able to compartmentalize your expression and your performance. On the positive side, if you have had glowing reviews in the past this will reinforce for the company the need to try to retain you.

2. Company culture

    a. Is the culture of the workplace progressive or conservative?

    b. Are you in an industry like academia, technology, or media, which is usually more progressive; or science, finance, or sales, which can be more conservative?

c. Do your corporate leaders value diversity and inclusion across race, religion, gender, gender identity, and sexual expression?

d. Is there an HR department? If your company has one, not only are the staff there expected to help you manage your transition, but they are also responsible for addressing the concerns of others who may react to your transition. Understanding this dual role requires empathy and an open mind on your part.

e. Does your company have a diversity and inclusion group, which is usually part of the HR department?

f. Does your company have harassment and discrimination guidelines and training?

g. Do you know of any gender non-conforming or LGBTQ+ co-workers? Sometimes knowledge of others like you in the company will make it more comfortable for you to decide to come out.

h. Is there an LGBTQ+ employee group? Your company might sponsor a formal LGBTQ+ support group or have created an ally system. In a 2013 survey by the Center for Talent Innovation,[1] nearly a quarter of LGBTQ+ workers believed that having a strong network of allies at work convinced them to come out. You don't even have to come out to enquire about or be connected to a support group. Some employers run support groups for family members, friends, or colleagues of LGBTQ+ employees, where discretion is a key feature.

i. Are there any "out" LGBTQ+ top executives or members of senior management in your organization?

---

1   www.talentinnovation.org/_private/assets/PowerOfOut-2-ExecSumm-CTI.pdf.

3. Related issues

    a. How connected are your family and work lives?

    b. Are you socially friendly with any of your co-workers outside the office or beyond office functions?

I thought I knew the answers to these questions for my situation. Even though the company was a leader in creating medications that served the LGBTQ+ community, when I was confronted about my change in appearance they had no LGBTQ+ policies in place beyond generic anti-discrimination and anti-harassment training, which was required by law in California. Knowing that my company had no specific LGBTQ+ support was one of the reasons why I was not exactly ready to disclose my intention to transition when I was put on the spot that day. I did not declare at the time of my choosing. If HR hadn't challenged me about my nail polish and earrings, I probably would have waited another month or so to announce my intention to transition.

If your company's leaders are inclusive and value diversity, then that sets the tone for everybody else in the organization as to what behaviors will be modeled and expected. One way to assess this is to look at your company's website. See if the company posts specific non-discriminatory language, or has clear policies or codes of conduct. If it does, then at the very least there's a much better chance that it is actually an open environment. This is the best-case scenario: a company that formally acknowledges that transgender and gender-diverse employees have the right to be who they are, openly, just like everyone else, which includes expressing their gender identity without fear of adverse consequences in the workplace. Similarly, the company has the right to expect that employees support the needs of the business to function smoothly. I interviewed other transgender individuals working at some of the most progressive companies and learned that those companies even offered specific educational and training sessions around transgender issues timed to coincide with an employee's announcement to transition, which generally made the whole process even smoother.

If there is nothing posted on the website, understand that, for the most part, companies want to do the right thing and assume good intent. They may not be expecting your announcement, and they may not know what to do for you, but that doesn't mean that they will be unwilling to work with you. If you really like your job and like your company, give it the benefit of the doubt.

However, a lack of knowledge about transgender and gender non-conforming issues within any company has the potential for creating misunderstanding and tension. While it should not be your responsibility to raise the consciousness of your entire office, in reality, you may have to pave the way for your company to adjust to your transition. This book can be a primary resource, and there are other established options that can help you create a more inclusive environment for yourself and other LGBTQ+ workers. For instance, Out & Equal is a workplace advocacy group which has developed *Gender Identity and Transition Guidelines*. A copy of the guidelines can be found on its website at http://outandequal. org/app/uploads/2016/09/Transition-Guidelines-Full-Edition.pdf. Organizations like Trans*formation (www.transformationuk.com) and TransCanWork (http://transcanwork.org) provide training services and networking events specifically for companies, large and small.

Corporate best practices: spotlight on Dow Chemical

Today, there are more than a handful of companies that are coming forward and creating formalized transgender transition protocols. These are typically industry leaders and are setting a nice pace for everyone else who, it is hoped, will follow. After reviewing many of these guidelines, I have found them to be remarkably similar. Therefore, these best practices can be standardized, and adopted by any size company, from a major corporation to a small business with a handful of employees. A well-developed transition plan is based on mutual respect for the transitioning or gender fluid employee, their co-workers, customers, business partners, and management. Such a plan helps all affected parties successfully navigate the transition and contributes to the company's ability to diminish or eliminate workflow disruptions.

For instance, Dow Chemical, which has 56,000 employees and is based in Midland, Michigan, is one of the companies I met with that has formalized transition guidelines. According to Cory Valente, PhD, who is part of its HR department, the corporate culture is very affirming. The guidelines state that transgender employees have the right to discuss their gender identity or expression openly, or to keep that information private. Only the transgender employee can decide when or whether to disclose private information. The employee's manager, HR support, or co-workers should not disclose information that may reveal an employee's transgender status or gender non-conforming presentation to others. This kind of personal or confidential information may only be shared with the transgender employee's consent and with co-workers who truly need to know to perform their jobs.

An employee has the right to be addressed by the employee's preferred name and by pronouns (for example, he, she, they) and other terms of address consistent with their gender identity. A court-ordered name change or other official documentation is not required.

Employees who transition on the job can expect the support of Dow Chemical's management and HR staff. The HR manager works with each transitioning employee individually to ensure a successful workplace transition. Dow recommends that transitioning employees work with managers to develop a workplace transition plan that addresses some issues that may occur during an employee's transition. This workplace transition plan should be developed individually with each transitioning employee and their HR manager to meet their specific needs.

Before the workplace transition begins, the transitioning employee meets with their HR representative to inform management

Making Your Initial Declaration

of the upcoming transition. The HR representative then informs the employee about the company's transgender-related policies and the availability of transition-related healthcare benefits. Next, a meeting is scheduled between the transitioning employee, the employee's supervisor, the HR representative, and other company representatives, such as members of the company's LGBTQ+ support group, if desired by the transitioning employee, to ensure the supervisor knows of the employee's planned transition. Other management members who interact with the employee should be made aware of the employee's planned transition so that leaders can express their support when the employee's transition is made known to the employee's work team. This will be done by HR with the approval of the transitioning employee. During this first team meeting or at subsequently scheduled meetings, a timeframe for the employee's transition process is developed, as it is likely that not all individuals of the transition team need to be brought on board at once.

At that point, Dow believes that each transgender individual should come up with their own plan for making the transition known at work. One employee may prefer a quick start in which all their co-workers and peers are informed about the transition at the end of the working week, and the employee makes the transition to their new gender expression in the workplace the following week. Another employee may prefer a more gradual transition, in which colleagues are notified of the transition, but the employee will not actually present in the new gender role until a later date. However, the company does require setting a formal date for when the change in gender expression will officially occur. This means the date that the employee will change their gender expression, name, and pronouns, and begin using the bathrooms for their desired gender identity.

The official notification may be done in person or via email from the supervisor. A link to additional resources and optional training offered can also be provided if the team is geographically dispersed or it is determined that an in-person meeting is not feasible. The transitioning employee may choose not to attend; however, it is mandatory for the supervisor, HR leader(s), and a member from the ethics and compliance team to be there to answer questions and explain Dow's non-discrimination policies.

The HR department then decides what, if any, training will be given to the transitioning employee's co-workers. At the same time, they work with the transitioning employee to determine dates of any leave that may be needed for scheduled medical procedures.

On the first day of the employee's official workplace transition, the transitioning employee should be welcomed in the same manner as an employee who has been newly hired or transferred.

This includes making sure that the transitioning employee has a new ID badge and photo if necessary, ensuring all work documents have the appropriate name and gender and checking that these have been updated in all of the places and systems where an employee's name may appear.

As a best practice, both the direct manager and the HR manager involved with the transition should visit with the employee formally approximately one month after transition.

MORE SUPPORT FROM INTEL

Intel has developed a formalized process that provides for effective communications and minimizes disruptions to the workplace which is very similar to the Dow Chemical approach. One additional policy it puts in place protects the employee during the transition. In Intel's words:

> During the transition period an employee may be living one gender in their personal life and another in their work life. During the transition period, the employee may present either gender at work. The employee is treated in accordance to the gender they present when they report to work. Intel may not require an employee to choose.

Meet Charles Burkard at Salesforce

Salesforce, one of the world's most successful customer relationship management platforms, includes industry-leading services spanning sales, service, marketing, commerce, communities, collaboration, and industries. It is based in San Francisco, California, and employs roughly 30,000 individuals as of 2018. The company is committed to equality for all, including the LGBTQ+ community, and recently hosted the Transform Tech Conference, the first summit for transgender and gender non-conforming people in technology. According to the company's website, it strives to be a place where everyone can bring their full, authentic self to work and feel supported. Salesforce strives to create workplaces that reflect the communities it serves and where everyone feels empowered to bring their full, authentic selves to work.

Charles Burkard's experience was completely in line with Salesforce's mission and values. As he stated on an interview posted on its website:

> I joined the Salesforce family as a Technical Support Engineer just over six years ago, and there isn't a day that goes by that I'm not grateful for our relationship. A little over a year ago I decided it was time to make a major change in my life, a change I had always wanted to make, but didn't have the resources or guidance at the time to take the leap. I was ready to transition from female to male identifying. ... I wanted the world to see me as I have always seen myself. I dove in and read every article and piece of documentation I could get my hands on. I worked with my partner to understand how the change would impact her and our relationship. I met other trans men that had already transitioned to get their thoughts on the experience. I confided in friends to gauge their reaction so I could ready myself. I was lucky enough to feel my friends and family would be accepting. ... My workplace was the only area in my life where I felt trepidation. How would this impact the relationships I had spent

years building? How would my manager react? Would he treat me differently? What would my VPs and executives say? What if I ran into a customer who I had worked with as "Christine" who wouldn't understand that now I am Charles and use he/him pronouns? Would someone challenge me? How would I handle that? Would my name be able to get updated in our internal systems?

I knew that for me, the first place to start was with my manager. I nervously told him my intentions and concerns, and he handled this entirely new situation beautifully. We talked about the team and how to communicate about my transformation. We researched and found guidance for the process and worked with our Employee Success team to make a plan. He was incredibly supportive and it reassured me. I felt the best way to announce this news [to the rest of the company] was to post to my profile on Chatter, our internal social network. I felt it was important to create a safe forum for conversation. I welcomed questions, but made sure to discern the difference between appropriate and inappropriate questions. I offered insight into how important this change was to me, hoping to instill that importance in others. My goal was to foster an opportunity for awareness and education, and I feel I was successful. I was met with excitement, congratulations, support and encouragement. People had questions, but no one ever crossed the line of professionalism. Of course, people would slip up and say "Christine" or "she," but would immediately apologize and correct themselves.

...It was everyone's unwavering support and care that made my experience completely positive. There were no difficult conversations, no alienation, no negativity. ... Post-transition, I have found that I am more confident and comfortable in myself and in my role. I feel I finally have the voice I've been seeking because I feel secure in who I am and what I have to contribute. I consider myself extremely fortunate to work for a company that is so inclusive and has such a strong stance on equality.

My declaration

Once I made up my mind during the hours after I was approached by the HR department about the earrings and nail polish, my attorney and I agreed I would draft an email in which I would state my situation and intentions, and I would send it to the HR representative and my boss. Then I would go tell my boss personally.

Here is the email I sent to the HR employee who confronted me:

Although we spoke a bit around the issue of my appearance, I need to let you know what is going on. For longer than I care to recall I have been playing a role in terms of gender identity. While I have presented as a man, my self-perception is that I am a woman. I have been "out" as a woman in certain contexts for quite a while, but am only now finding that I cannot, consistent with my psychological balance, continue to pretend at work that my gender identity is male.

With our discussion this morning, it is apparent that I need to make my situation clear to the company, or at least to those in the company who need to (or perceive a need to) know what is going on with me. You have suggested that I may not be comfortable remaining here (or, if I understand correctly, that others may not be comfortable with my remaining here). I have been uncomfortable presenting as a man (as opposed to a woman) for many years. I am committed to our company and to my profession. Whether I identify or present as a man or a woman does not and will not make any difference with respect to my commitment or my ability to perform my job. My skill set, knowledge base and abilities have not changed. I have no wish nor intention to leave.

I am happy to work with you, with other parts of HR, and with [my boss] to make my transition in a manner that will cause the least disruption or discomfort in the workplace. The company is large enough and mature enough (and, I am confident, my colleagues are generous enough and mature enough) to accommodate my gender identity and the process of transition. As I transition to presenting as a woman, I will strive to present myself in a manner consistent with the general ways in which other women in the workplace dress and present themselves. I will be business appropriate in my attire. I do understand that my transition process will be noticed. I know that it is not the usual thing.

I've been here long enough and have enough confidence in my co-workers to believe that any distraction will be short-lived and will not interfere with the company's operations. I look to you and HR for understanding and assistance to help me (and my co-workers) through this process. I plan to meet with [my boss] personally at 3pm today to inform him as well.

Thanks,

Dave

Immediately after sending that email I strode up to speak with my boss. I sat down in his office and said I had something personal to discuss with him. I didn't know how aware he might have been about the situation with HR from earlier in the day, but I proceeded as if he did not know. I also had brought a hard copy of the email I just sent to him and to HR with me.

I related the conversation with HR, and then I said, "I realized I was transgender and I intend to transition at work." That exact wording became a key message point, which I repeated many times later on when I was announcing my decision to my people and others in the communication cascade.

In my discussions with him I made sure to not appear as though I was unsure about my decision or that I had been grappling with an identity "problem" or "issue." I thought it was essential that I convey my decision as one that was not attached to any negative context.

My boss seemed very surprised by my revelation. He had known I was recently divorced but did not seem to be concerned about my appearance. He actually said he had not been aware of my earlier conversation with HR, which I found a bit disingenuous since I doubted HR would do something like that without his knowledge. He said he had noticed my change in appearance but said he thought

I was just "running with a different crowd" like musicians or another more edgy group since my divorce.

Since he was a bit taken aback by my news and was usually a man of few words, he suggested that we should keep this conversation to ourselves and I should work with HR to plan how this transition could happen. I agreed to do that and said I would refrain from wearing the earrings and polish for now while we put the plan in place, since I wanted to avoid any additional problems. So, I stepped back into the closet and shut the door again for the next two months.

When I got back to my desk I received the following response to my email from HR:

Hi Dave,

Thank you for sharing this very personal information; it's very much appreciated and please know that myself and "HR" will work with you through this transition. I would like to clarify that in no way was I intending to imply that others may not be comfortable with you remaining [here]; that given what was known when we spoke this morning it was regarding expectations at the senior leadership/VP levels with regard to decorum. Of course, with this different information you have our support to work through this with you with complete understanding for all concerned.

Look forward to talking soon.

Her tune had changed dramatically in just a few hours because I had declared I was transgender, and now was a member of a "protected class." However, this email response from HR did have an unfortunate consequence. My administrative assistant, who was fantastic and who I trusted completely with all aspects of my workplace life, was not aware of my gender decision, but she had access to my emails. As soon as I saw the response I tried to remove it from my inbox and hoped that she had not seen it since I would have wanted to tell her personally. Unfortunately, she had seen it and I did not have a chance to talk with her privately until several days later when we were both in the office.

The next time I was in the office I apologized for the fact that she had found out about my situation that way. I told how I had arrived at my decision to transition, what was agreed with my boss and how I would be working on the communication plan. I told her that I hoped she would want to continue to work for me but that if she was uncomfortable I would understand. Although I did not express any doubts to her about my expectations to stay with the company, I was concerned that if I had conveyed any uncertainty about the future she may also be worried about her own future employment, and I did not want her to worry. Over the next few weeks there did seem to be a distance between us which had not existed before, and I viewed it as the first instance of collateral damage related to my coming out. But fortunately, within a few months, my relationship with my administrative assistant returned to our usual close camaraderie and she became an invaluable supporter of me and my transition.

Because I was the first employee at the company to transition in a decade, HR brought in an outside HR consultant who had worked with other companies. I was disappointed that our internal HR department had absolutely no background in this situation, but it was reassuring that the consultant was experienced. He reassured us that transitions almost always go well. In his experience, he had found that co-workers are usually very supportive and can help foster an inclusive and accepting climate if they are informed. He also told me that my transition was mine to share—I needed to decide how and what to tell them.

After that meeting, I realized that HR's role would be one of support. They would help me communicate my plan to a small group prior to my initial broad announcement. They had no useful advice about the actual content of my communication, and seemed more worried about how my co-workers would react rather than what I was going through. However, I had to accept that and I prepared to move forward.

Other people's experiences

By and large, many individuals who have transitioned at larger companies have had very supportive help from their HR departments and senior managers. For instance, when Dr. Renee McLaughlin of Cigna Insurance met with HR after deciding to transition, she had intended to resign, but her HR contact convinced her to stay. I heard very positive stories from people who transitioned at or currently work for companies such as HSBC, Intel, Lockheed Martin, and Facebook. These companies encourage and celebrate diversity and inclusion and have well-established transition guidelines that closely resemble the ones I have included in this chapter.

Depending on the culture and type of business that you are in, even a small company can be very progressive and supportive. However, if you find yourself in a company that is not well versed in diversity, it may fall on you to educate them and your co-workers in preparation for your transition. As you've learned, there are many groups that can help you be not only an advocate for yourself, but for diversity in general.

The next step

Once my boss and HR knew my intentions, it became very obvious that I needed to create a plan to tell everyone else I worked with. It's rare, and probably not a very good idea, for anyone who is transitioning to take a two-week vacation and come back with an entirely different gender expression without telling their co-workers ahead of time. In the next chapter, I'll explain how I did this successfully with my 400+ employees.

CHAPTER 5

INFORMING COLLEAGUES AND CUSTOMERS

Your communication plan needs to be as carefully planned as every other aspect of your transition. The goal is to craft a message that leaves the recipient with a positive and reassuring attitude toward you and tries to minimize discomfort and uncertainty. Once the message is created, it can be used for a variety of audiences, including HR, management, colleagues, and customers.

Your talking points should directly reflect how you feel about your transition. Your colleagues should feel how you feel: that you are positive and excited, as well as grounded, at peace, and doing the right thing. You also want to stay away from engaging in stereotypes that portray transgender individuals as having a sickness or furthering the mis-impression that gender dysphoria is a self-created problem that they're going to need to adjust to because of you.

Your emotions or inconsistencies with your language will make people feel those same emotions, and it will be harder for them to support you. As I was crafting my language, I never referred to my transition negatively. I did not use words like "problem," "issue," or "diagnosis," when describing changing gender identity. Instead, I used words like "realization," "revelation," and "recognition." These words create a less negative context: in essence you are saying that the transition is part of your own personal journey that might touch their world in an indirect way. I was trying to convey that I had made a deliberate decision that I was happy about, and that I was looking forward to being the same person I always was, just with a new outward appearance.

This approach is a leadership technique that pays off. What you're trying to do is remove as much of other people's discomfort as you can by making them feel that as many unknowns as possible have been addressed so they can move on with the new you in a direction that is clear. This way, you leave little option but to be treated fairly.

I also was very careful not to make jokes or make light of the situation. While it would be tempting to use humor to reduce anxiety, especially early on when you are newly presenting in your new persona, a transition is a serious decision. I was worried that my attempt at humor would make me seem less serious about the importance of the changes I would be going through. For instance, there were more than a few times that the word transition was used in workplace discussions, usually in relation to changes in the business climate or processes. I could have made a comment such as "Since I know a lot about transitions…" or something to that effect, but I never wanted to refer to my gender transition in an offhand manner.

My experience

Your approach will be dependent on the types and categories of people you work with, including your customers outside your workplace. When I transitioned, I was a senior executive and managed more than 400 employees across 30 countries.

My approach was to tell my direct reports and their teams in my office personally that I was going to transition before I had my first scheduled surgery. I could have just made a broad communication over email or allowed HR to send out the news, but that wasn't my preference. I felt that my change in gender expression wasn't a business decision, yet it affected all of my co-workers. I also realized that this change was out of the ordinary for the typical workplace. And because it was the manifestation of a personal rather than a business decision and wasn't at all related to the work that my co-workers or I did, I felt that it warranted a personal communication directly from me as to why I was making this change, and when it was going to happen. I wanted to create the least amount of disruption and to give my best explanation as to how and why they would be impacted. I had an incredible amount of respect for my team and realized that I was asking a lot for them to maintain their usual high performance as their leader changed so dramatically.

I worked with HR to create a timeline where I informed colleagues in similar groups, so everyone in a particular subset was on the same page at the same time. We worked backwards from my first planned appearance in the office as Dana. I scheduled my first facial feminization surgery for May 26, the Tuesday after Memorial Day, and I would be out for three weeks and therefore return to work in mid-June.

I had been thinking about my message and practicing the delivery for two-and-a-half months. I memorized this speech so well that every time I needed to tell someone, the message came out in a very similar way. My speech had five key elements in order to make sure that everyone got the same communication and, I hope, took away the same messages:

- I have recently realized I am transgender and have decided to transition at work, and when I return from surgery in mid-June I will be my preferred self.

- I am really happy about my plans.

- I know everyone will behave as consummate professionals and continue to do an excellent job at their work.

- People should not worry about using the wrong pronouns or slipping up with my old name.

- If anyone has any questions or wants to talk about it privately, my door is open.

I had previously scheduled 40 of my senior leaders from all over the world to come to the home office for an important meeting about our future as a group in mid-April. This extended leadership meeting had been planned for nearly a year and was crucial for the organization to align and agree on our priorities for successfully leading the organization in the future. I decided that I did not want to inform them about my transition at that time since it would overshadow the objectives of the meeting. True to my character and my beliefs about my responsibilities to the company as their leader, I was committed to achieving the intended goals of the meeting without any distractions.

After the extended senior leadership meeting in April, the stage was set for the communication plan to begin. The communication roll-out plan was as follows: I would first meet with the most senior person in my department—the Chief Scientific Officer who was head of research and development and reported directly to the Chief Executive Officer (CEO)—to get his support, and simultaneously HR would approach the CEO to make sure there were no concerns from him. Because there were no policies in place, HR felt it was important for me to be able to say in subsequent communications that senior executive management was supportive.

The head of research and development was a brilliant scientist and HR had set me up a meeting with him without providing any topic, so he had no idea what I would say. The HR department had been very good about holding my information confidential between, them, my boss, the consultant, and my assistant. I was extremely nervous because this meeting would set the tone for the rest of the communication roll-out as well as my future in the organization.

I started the conversation by telling him I had recently been divorced and had done some serious soul searching around potential factors in that, but then went to my five key messages. When I told him I wanted to transition at work he said, "Oh, is that all? I thought you were going to tell me you were going to resign and go live in the woods or something."

He then asked a lot of questions around the medical aspects of the transition, which I answered. His interest in what was facing me and some of the details of a transition actually comforted me in that he seemed to care about what I would be going through. I was very relieved and encouraged. He asked me to move as quickly as I could through my communication plan and suggested a few additional people he wanted me to speak to personally.

The next step was to tell my eight direct reports individually, and we would discuss how to disseminate the news to their teams. In each conversation, I worked through the same five elements and tried to make sure people felt comfortable enough to ask me questions if they had them. I was able to talk directly and in person to the five who worked in my office building, and I told the remaining three who were not located in the company headquarters personally over the phone.

All of my direct reports were very surprised at the news but were also immediately supportive. During each conversation, we discussed how we would share the information with their individual teams—they could do it or I would do it. I left the decision up to them and offered to meet with their teams personally if they preferred. I told them that if they decided to tell their teams themselves, they needed to make sure they said I was very happy about the change and that if their employees had any questions they could come to see me personally.

After the initial notifications to my direct reports, I received one very nice note from one of them, who had worked for me since I had started at the company.

Hi Dave,

Thank you for sharing your news. I absolutely respect your personal decision and look forward to our continued close collaboration and the positive working relationship that I have enjoyed over the past eight years.

With my sincere best wishes,

Paul

Two of my direct reports who worked in my office complex chose to tell their teams themselves. The other three requested that I tell their teams. A few of the teams were moderate in size and some were quite large, so in order to reach them all we broke the larger groups into parts. We then scheduled one or two team meetings a day over the next three days for those direct reports who preferred that I did the communication to their teams.

The first meeting was on a Monday afternoon with a group of approximately 20 people. I walked in and took a seat at the head of the table. As I had with the individual meetings, I started by saying that I had experienced a lot of personal changes over the last year with a separation and divorce which had led to a bit of soul searching and personal assessment. I realized I was transgender and decided to transition at work. I would be going out for surgery but when I came back I would be the preferred me and I was really excited about it. I told them I would be happy to talk to any of them personally if they had questions or that they could also talk to HR if they felt they needed to. I stopped there and took a deep breath, waiting for the reaction. I was shocked when I actually got a round of applause! I had hoped it would go well but never expected that.

All the subsequent meetings went just as well, although I didn't get more applause. After that very first meeting, I started to get personal emails from members of my larger staff, which all voiced support or admiration for my decision and my willingness to be vulnerable and tell them personally. Those notes were incredibly affirming; here are some of the ones I've held on to.

Dear Dave,

Thank you for sharing your news with us today in Regulatory Affairs CMC [a group that works with documentation for manufacturing of drugs]. I'm very happy for you and wish you all the best in this new chapter of life. It is really inspiring to work with someone that is true to themselves and faces such situations with so much courage.

Looking forward to seeing the new you!

Kind Regards,

Sita

★ ★ ★

It was a brave thing you did and in my opinion only a woman can do that ☺.

Take care of yourself and wish you all the best!

Kind Regards,

Farzaneh

★ ★ ★

Dear Dana,

Thank you for taking the time to speak with the Hepatitis C Virus team this morning. I know you are very busy and we all really appreciate your willingness to take the time to share such a personal journey with us. It's rare for leaders to open up and allow their vulnerability to show and it has been incredible to hear your story and see the example you are setting for us.

This week has been so valuable for me as I've taken a moment to realize what a special team we have. I feel so fortunate to work with such trusting and open colleagues.

Have a great weekend! ☺

Michele

★ ★ ★

Hi Dave/Dana

Thank you for sharing your touching story and your plan to transition. It's great that you are doing this. I'm happy that you will be able to become the person you truly want to be soon. Good luck with everything. If there's anything you need, please don't hesitate to let me know.

All the best,

Greena (Attorney/Editor Medical Writing Group)

★ ★ ★

I just wanted to write a quick note to thank you for that meeting. It was very courageous and moving. You handled it admirably. I also wanted to congratulate you on not just recognizing, but realizing your true gender identity and moving forward with the change that this brings to your life. You certainly have my support and best wishes.

Take care,

Liam (Regulatory Systems Group)

The positive feedback continued as I told our European divisions during one mammoth conference call, since word from the smaller group meetings at headquarters had started to leak out, and there was no way I could reach the international employees in person in face-to-face meetings. Because of the time difference, I made the call from home early in the morning. When I arrived at work, my administrative assistant, who had been there for about a half hour, said to me, "Have you seen your email? I have tears in my eyes." While I was getting to work I had received numerous congratulatory and appreciative emails from my European colleagues who were on the call. This was very gratifying, and I breathed a sigh of relief that I was getting such positive reactions.

During the next two weeks that led up to my surgery, I made the rounds with others in the head office that I needed to inform before I returned as Dana. One of the most positive interactions occurred when I went to talk to the head of Treasury who had previously invited me to accompany him on a business trip in August. I had accepted the invitation, but now felt I should let him know about my transition which would take place before the trip. What's more, he was also going to supervise my son Nick during an internship in his department that summer, so I especially wanted to get my news to him quickly. I didn't know how he would react, whether he might not want me on the trip, and whether it might have negative repercussions for my son. But when I stopped by his office and told him the news, he was very positive and said it was great that I was doing it and by all means they still wanted me on the trip in August. He confided that he knew a high school classmate, who had been the captain of the football team, and who had later transitioned. She was now a documentary film maker and he had just seen her at their high school reunion!

The supportive role HR can play

If your company has an HR department, an HR staff member should work with you to ensure a successful workplace transition. The HR representative should be able to tell you about the company's policies regarding changing names on documents or credentials, and the availability of transition-related healthcare benefits. You can then develop a timeline for your transition, including your communication plan and any time out of the office you will require.

In my case, there were no policies related to healthcare benefits to discuss, since the company specifically excluded transgender healthcare from its benefits package. I had learned this when my surgeon's office had tried to obtain approval from Anthem Blue Cross, which did cover these benefits for companies who chose to include them in their employee health coverage.

However, HR felt they might need to provide support to any employees who had questions or may be uncomfortable after I had announced my intention to transition, which I thought was a good idea. To the best of my knowledge, I never heard of anyone in the office who had any reason to talk with HR about my transition or complained about working with me. I attributed this positive environment to the way that I handled the initial communication roll-out and the efforts that I made to personally communicate my news as much as possible.

HR should also support you if you feel you are being harassed, particularly if someone in the office refuses to address you by your preferred gender identity. If it is deliberate, this is one of the most common forms of discrimination.

Dealing with feedback

There's a common saying among transgender individuals that you are not transitioning alone, but you are taking everyone else along with you. Whether they are family, friends, co-workers, or acquaintances, everyone has to adjust to your transition. They do it in different ways and at different times. It is a big challenge to try to anticipate those different reactions and varying paces of acceptance. Some people are going to immediately embrace your news. Others are going to be a little standoffish. There are people who are not going to look at you the same way. Then there are people who will surprise you with an outpouring of positivity.

Your communication plan needs to take the feedback you'll receive into account, so that you can mentally prepare for it.

According to Victoria Datta, another pharmaceutical executive and writer on the website www.trans.cafe, adjust your expectations by giving people space and be patient—even the best intentioned may not get pronouns and names right in the beginning. Open yourself up to questions, remembering that you may be the only trans person your co-workers know. And, be mentally prepared for the worst to happen, such as someone walking out of a meeting or dismissing you with a hurtful comment.

There will always be people who will have difficulties accepting the new you, and this may come across in different ways. For instance, while HR always seemed to be on board before my transition, my boss was less supportive and empathetic. In the two-month gap between the time I first declared my intention to transition and the time I left the office for the first surgery, I would meet periodically with my boss, just as we had always done. I would update him on what was happening in my department and get his input on various issues. During one of these one-on-one meetings, I offered to brief him on my upcoming communication plan: the roll-out to tell the rest of my colleagues what would be happening. At the time, my boss didn't seem particularly interested and said, "It's your show." I didn't react outwardly but was surprised and offended by that remark, and thought it was derisive and demeaning. To me, it showed that he thought my transition was more of a performance than a life-changing identity affirmation.

After the full communication roll-out, one of my work friends reacted in a way I wasn't expecting. Before I transitioned, Steve and I were close. We grabbed lunch together occasionally, and talked about sports, particularly the Golden State Warriors. Yet, after my transition, Steve stopped engaging with me in any kind of conversation. While he wasn't critical to my success in the office, I can't pretend that his standoffishness didn't bother me. I never pressed the issue with him, because at some point I realized he wasn't essential to my job. Plus, I realized that if people didn't like me before I transitioned, my announcement would be another reason that they might not like me. However, if they always liked me, then they would probably not have a problem with it. Steve may have never liked me as much as I enjoyed his company. And ultimately, I accepted it, because his less than positive reaction was more than offset by so many more positive and even celebratory attitudes from my other co-workers.

GOOD MANNERS GO A LONG WAY

Once you come out, don't underestimate the fact that there will be an adjustment period for everyone in the office, including yourself. The more people you can personally bring on board during this time, the better. Keep your co-workers informed of major milestones in your transition, especially upcoming medical appointments. Otherwise, they may think something else is wrong when you are out of the office for a few weeks without notice. And, whenever someone sends you a supportive note, even if it's a text message, make sure to thank the person directly. Every time you do, you expand your support network.

The worst-case scenario: dealing with the idea of betrayal

I believe the underlying issue that prevents some people from embracing your authentic self is a feeling of betrayal. They view the situation as if you had a secret that you didn't want to share. Even though they may be hurt, you can explain that it wasn't personal, and that you were not specifically excluding them as you worked through your experience. You can say, "This situation was something that was so bottled up inside me that I wasn't sure what I was going to do until recently. I had to approach it systematically and now I'm ready to share my secret and my decision."

The next step

The next step for me was to take my first medical leave. I was out of the office for three weeks as I recovered from facial feminization surgery. This surgery represented an obvious change in my appearance, and it seemed like a good time to completely change my gender expression from male to female. Before I left I had decided that when I returned, I would be officially known at work as Dana. For me, that change included a radical departure from what I looked like before, and entailed growing my hair out, wearing makeup, getting a new wardrobe, and being mindful of my voice and body language.

The steps you take to mark your own transition are only for you to decide. Whether or not you choose to have surgery, or whether your previous gender expression was strongly at one end of the binary spectrum or the other, or somewhere in the middle, you will decide when you want to be officially recognized as the new you. And you will decide how the new you will show up at work. Whatever decisions you make, they will be right for you.

CHAPTER 6

GETTING READY FOR THE FIRST DAY BACK

The first day back to work as the new you is obviously going to be a big day. It's as if you're the star at a movie premiere: you are walking down the proverbial red carpet and everyone really is staring at you. It's a very exciting time, but it's also nerve-racking. So as with everything else about your transition, my advice is to prepare well in advance. This time, you are going to focus on how you want to look, and the changes you want to make to your behaviors that best match your chosen gender expression.

As excited and happy as I was that my outward appearance was beginning to reflect exactly how I felt about myself, I was also very stressed about going back to work, almost like a teenager being dropped off at a new school. It was as though I was compressing all of the "how do I look" feelings of adolescence, young adulthood, and early workplace anxieties into the run-up to one single day. I wanted to make sure that my gender expression matched my gender identity: my hair, makeup, and clothes all had to be right.

I decided to dress a bit more formally, because I was treating my return almost like a very important job interview. I realized that in some ways coming back to the office would be like starting all over again, and I wanted to create a good first impression as Dana. I thought through each of my presentation decisions very carefully, especially my clothes.

I knew that my colleagues would have a wide range of expectations regarding my appearance. People would certainly be imagining me to look different, since I had told them I was going to be out of the office for surgery. Even though I didn't widely share the specifics of the facial feminization procedure, I worried that the people in my office expected me to return looking like Cher or Joan Rivers. The truth was I just looked like a more feminine version of myself. Before the surgery, I asked my surgeon how he would describe the effect of the facial feminization procedure. He explained that the surgery would be as if he had turned me into my sister. There would still be a lot of similarities remaining between my old and new selves, especially my eyes and my smile.

The surgery was very painful, and the recovery took a long time—it was a week before all the stitches came out and a full three weeks before all swelling subsided and the bruising cleared. But I made good use of this time. I spent hours practicing how I would apply my makeup, how I would style my hair, exploring my intended clothing style, and working on a more feminine way of walking and talking. I shopped one last time for my office clothing about a week before my debut. My goal was to be as completely convincing as possible.

While I was recovering, I spent a great deal of time worrying about "passing." This is a major anxiety for anyone who wants to transition, especially when you first present yourself in the office. Passing refers to a transgender person's ability to be correctly perceived as the gender they identify with, and at the same time, to not be perceived as transgender. During my time off work when I was recovering from my surgery, I often worried whether I would ever be accepted and seen by others as a woman.

Within the trans community, especially in blogs online, you may come across the words "passing privilege" which refers to trans people who have the added protection of not appearing trans. There's a good reason for noting this distinction. Trans people who aren't perceived as being transgender experience significantly less harassment than trans people who are visibly trans.

The truth is, some in the trans community pass better than others, and the factors that go into this ability include age and financial resources. We also know the saying, "Trans men can pass in the streets but not in the sheets," which basically means that they can pass, even androgynously, without much effort, in the outside world. The situation is just the opposite for MTF transitions: it's harder for trans women to pass in the streets, but not in the sheets if you have gender-affirming surgery.

People who transition at a younger age are frequently better at passing if hormone blockers are administered during puberty to prevent the development of secondary sex characteristics like breasts or facial hair. But in the case of transitioning adults, not every trans person can afford surgery or hormone therapies, making passing more difficult. What's more, there are some aspects of your physical self that no amount of money or surgery will change. For instance, I'm a five-foot ten-inch trans woman, so am fairly tall for a woman, and there is absolutely nothing I can do that will make me shorter. When I look in the mirror I feel as if I must *stand out* to a certain extent, and my worry at one point was that once you stand out with one aspect of how you present to others, people will pay more attention to your other physical attributes, and you will not "pass."

After two years of hormone therapy and three major surgeries, I realized that I had changed my outward appearance as much as I could and was going to have to be comfortable with how I looked. I began to realize that being trans was not a negative, it was who I was. Once I accepted that, I got over worrying about what other people thought. I realized that many trans women were as tall as I was, and I looked just as good, and passed just as effectively, as the average transgender woman in her 50s. I was never going to look like the best-looking 25-year-old but I was happy with who I was, the journey I had undertaken, and, most importantly, I was proud of the way I looked. It also didn't hurt that I was frequently asked for advice by other trans people or praised for my look and mannerisms.

Plan ahead for the big reveal

Everything about your new gender expression will take time, and you're not expected to come into work looking as if you've just won the Miss Universe pageant. There are certain aspects of your transition that will take considerable time to come to fruition, such as hormone therapy, hair removal, and voice training. You simply can't wait until the night before to get ready. Be patient, have a plan, and give yourself enough time to try different looks and practice with makeup and hairstyling.

Hormones take months to begin creating noticeable changes. Removing unwanted facial and body hair through laser therapy and electrolysis, as well as growing out your hair (for MTF) can take more than a year. These treatments can begin well in advance of your declaration and your first appearance as the new you at work. The further along you are in these areas the better it will be for changing your gender expression at work and for your first day back.

I started growing out my hair a full year before I officially changed my gender expression at work. I had worn my hair very short as a guy and I had been gray since my mid-30s. When I first started dressing as a woman outside work, I had to wear wigs and I tried them in different hairstyles and colors. Eventually I decided to grow my hair out and started working with Michelle, a very talented hairstylist. Since I was not out at work at the time, we had to come up with a plan that would be less obvious at work until I was ready to make my declaration. I went to see Michelle with my wig and she did an assessment of what might look good for me after my transition. I decided that I would still wear the wig when I was socializing as Dana, but she would style my hair so that I could neatly comb it back when I had to dress as David at work.

When I finally appeared for the first time as Dana in the office, my hair had grown out a bit but overall was still gray and pretty short for a woman. However, it was styled neatly and beginning to look feminine. Three years later, I can say that my hair is still a work in progress.

Once I transitioned, I decided to try some color while still allowing the hair to grow out. I even tried hair extensions when I was getting impatient—my hair just seemed to be taking too long to grow. However, the extensions required a lot of maintenance and were very expensive, so I eventually took them out. Two years later my hair has grown and I've adopted a flattering, feminine style for the blond hair I have now.

I also started laser hair removal immediately after making my decision to transition because it was one of the treatments I could completely control and it did not require a medical prescription. This was over a year before my change in gender expression at work. Laser hair removal is costly but very efficient and after several sessions it usually does a good job removing dark hair although it is not effective for light or gray hair. Unfortunately, I had a lot of gray, especially on my face, and I had to switch to electrolysis. Electrolysis is the painstaking process of applying electric current to individual hair follicles one at a time. Due to the rather slow growth cycles of hair follicles, it usually takes multiple treatments for either laser or electrolysis to stop hair growth permanently.

Today, electrolysis may be covered under your health insurance plan, but the number of sessions that are included (less than ten, according to some reports) is woefully inadequate. The truth is that electrolysis is a long, painful, and expensive process. I tried to do some intensive electrolysis on my face prior to my first facial surgery, subjecting myself to 13 hours a week of treatments for two weeks in a row. That intensive regimen took quite a toll on my skin—I had redness, tiny blisters, and temporary swelling and scarring since a strong electrical current is delivered to a small area of skin over too short a period of time. In retrospect, I should have factored in more time for electrolysis before scheduling the surgery. I am still receiving short, weekly electrolysis treatments (I refer to them as torture sessions) on my face and chest. Three years later I have very little regrowth on my face or chest and only spend about ten minutes a week having my meticulous electrologist zap the last few active beard follicles.

Put together an appropriate wardrobe

I also started planning my new wardrobe about a year in advance. As David, I always wore nicely tailored suits or designer casual clothes, but it took me a while to come up with Dana's equivalent office attire. I carefully watched the other women in my office for ideas. Then I worked with a personal shopper, and bought a variety of women's suits, slacks, and casual clothes. The casual outfits came together easily, but it took a little longer to find the right slacks and tops for work.

One of the first issues I had to deal with was simply the idea of going shopping for women's clothing. While shopping can be quite anonymous, I was not feeling that way at all. If an FTM trans person goes shopping in the men's department of Macy's or any other department store, the general public doesn't flinch. But a man looking at bras and panties (in his own size) at Victoria's Secret raises a few eyebrows.

I decided to use a free service many department stores offer—a stylist, otherwise known as a personal shopper. I made arrangements at two department stores—first Nordstrom and later on at the Barneys New York store in San Francisco. At the beginning, I agonized quite a bit about my first appointment since I wasn't even close to coming out and was perpetually worried about being recognized by a friend or co-worker. Even though I had lived close to one of the best Nordstrom stores in California, in Palo Alto, I felt that it was too risky because my family or friends also shopped there frequently and I didn't want to take any chances. Instead, I chose a smaller Nordstrom store that was closer to my office and where it was unlikely that I would run into anyone who knew me. This store didn't have as wide a selection of styles, but it was good enough to get started.

When I asked Aejaie (from Carla's) for shopping advice, she suggested that I only work with a woman stylist since they know how things should fit and what the essentials are. I screwed up my courage and called the Nordstrom store and asked to speak to a stylist. Maybe it was my voice but I was told that I would be assigned to a salesman named Chris in the men's department. When I inquired about working with someone who could do women's styles, the woman on the phone said Chris could work with either men or women. Not seeing any other way out of the situation, I decided to put Aejaie's advice aside and I set up a private meeting with Chris.

I arranged for us to meet at the store one evening after work. I was very uneasy because this would be one of the first times I was going to share my secret with a complete stranger outside the professional medical or psychology setting, or the trans friends I made at Carla's. I nervously met Chris for coffee as my male self. I whispered to him about my situation and mentioned that I had been advised to only work with a woman stylist, but he puffed out his chest and stated, "I am a gay man and know styles and have worked with both men and women so I think I can help you." We talked a bit about styles and what types of clothes I thought I was looking for, and we agreed to set up another appointment at the store. The plan was that I would come into the store and he would have a private dressing room set aside, where he would bring me clothing and shoes to try on without me having to shop on the sales floor.

I really didn't have any idea what my "look" was going to be, but Chris did an admirable job trying to understand what I was looking for and making suggestions that would flatter my body. That first day at Nordstrom I was like a kid in a candy store and was very excited that several things looked reasonably good on me, particularly jeans and leggings, which highlighted my long legs. And due to the fact that I was fairly thin at that time, weighing about 165 pounds, many of the items did fit reasonably well. I must have purchased 20 or 30 pieces, including shoes and even a woman's business suit, but there was no unifying style or look, so eventually much of it did go back (thank God for the very liberal Nordstrom returns policy!). Chris also introduced me to Jennifer, a very nice woman in the cosmetics department who made me up and taught me a lot about the basics of cosmetics.

Over the next few months I met with a few other personal shoppers, and each one understood my situation and seemed to really want to help. Nordstrom became my mainstay in terms of casual clothing, but probably the biggest leap forward for my style was when I started to go to Barneys in San Francisco. At the time, Barneys had just produced a mailer for a campaign where all of the models were transgender, so I thought it might be comfortable working with me. Later, I was told that one of those models had been sent to each of the Barneys stores to teach the staff about trans dos and don'ts. The corporate culture was obviously inclusive, and it made me very comfortable to shop there.

I first had shopped as a guy at Barneys with my ex-wife when she was looking for jewelry, and we had worked with Lisel who was a very good salesperson and had taken excellent care of us. I decided to approach Lisel, tell her about my plans to transition, and ask her if she could introduce me to a personal shopper there. She told me that she had a friend who was transgender and would be happy to help me. Then she introduced me to Ferdinand in shoes, Paul in handbags, Nancy in women's designer clothes, and Ivy in cosmetics.

Nancy Rogers Ray was a great judge of the different looks and which ones would suit my frame. Even though I am fairly tall for a woman and on the thinner side, I have big shoulders and ribcage, so not everything fit me well right off the rack. I also had no breasts since I had only recently started hormones. We started by thinking about size, and which designers cut with a roomier shoulder, or frequently used a loose sleeve. She let me take the lead on what I was comfortable with, what I wanted to spend, and how much privacy I needed or didn't need. I let her take the lead on helping me define my style.

Nancy was also great about building my confidence. She was constantly reminding me that every woman has to pay more attention to certain parts of her body and has to "work with what she has." She helped me acquire a really nice wardrobe for work that could supplement what I had obtained (and not returned) from my shopping splurges at Nordstrom. Once we had a relationship going, I would call Nancy whenever I was planning to come into the store, and she would put outfits aside ahead of time, or order specific pieces in the right sizes that she thought would fit me but were not in stock at that store.

Those excursions to Barneys were very exciting and important to me early on. They offered me the chance to feel comfortable being out in public as Dana as I made my way around the city. I can still remember the exhilaration and fluttering in my stomach as I set out from my apartment, thrilled to be finally dressing as a woman in public and making progress toward establishing my style and persona for the future. Even now, every time I walk toward the store I still get a twinge of excitement in my stomach, the same way a faint whiff of perfume brings back vivid memories of people and sensations years afterwards. At Barneys, I was unlikely to be recognized and it became a safe space to explore my feminine self. Nancy was absolutely wonderful to work with and we still laugh about those early days when I was endlessly trying things on and my wig would go flying off my head each time I took off a top or a sweater in the dressing room.

If you don't have access to a store that offers personal shoppers, you can do a light shop anywhere and check out the sales people on the floor, or call the store ahead of time and see if the store manager can recommend someone you can work with. I had some great relationships in my local Macy's when I went in for lingerie or sports clothes. Once I went shopping with another transgender friend and the saleswoman was great. Remember, most sales people work on commission, so they want to sell you something. And they want you to like the way you look, so that you come back again and don't return what you buy from them.

Another option is ordering clothes online. Although it sounds like an ideal choice if you are not out because you don't have to leave your home, I found that, at least at the beginning, I ended up sending most of what I bought online back because the fit wasn't right. It's extremely hard unless you know the merchandise ahead of time and have a good understanding of what suits your frame. That's where the personal shopper can help you rapidly acquire a wardrobe. You can try things on and accept or reject them immediately, and once the shopper sees what you like, there are things that you might not have considered, or you were not aware of, that the salesperson can bring to your attention. One other advantage of personal shoppers is that when you work with them for a period of time, they remember what you bought earlier and can pick new items which can be mixed and matched with the previous pieces to increase your fashion options.

Once you have established your look and you know about the styles and fit of certain brands, online shopping can be a much more productive option. Knowing about a website's refund policy in advance is important. Some retailers like Zappos and Nordstrom are incredibly generous and understanding with respect to returns, but others are more restrictive.

Transgender specialty stores

Depending on where you live, another option is a specialty store that caters to cross-dressers and transgender clients. I had heard about Carla's Social Club and that's where I met Aejaie, who helped me so much in the early days. Even though it is located in San Jose, California, it has clients coming in from all over the world. What's special about Carla's is that Aejaie and some of the other employees are actually members of the trans community.

Aejaie told me that the majority of shoppers she meets with are MTF trans people. In her words, "They have the most needs when it comes to shopping and specific services like learning to apply makeup and do hair. They may also need wigs and undergarments, like bras and padded panties."

These speciality stores carry many items that you might want, such as lingerie and "foundational" undergarments, but I've found that their selection of everyday clothes is limited. These purchases are more important very early on when you are closeted and may not be ready to shop at mainstream stores in person or online. While these stores have an important place in the overall shopping experience, you can't rely on them exclusively.

THE MOST FAMOUS TRANS STORES

There are many online options for obtaining clothing and accessories for occasional cross-dressers and the trans community, and these can be an excellent resource for padded undergarments and breast forms. Among the most notable is the Michael Salem Boutique, which has been in business for nearly 50 years and has a physical location in New York City. The boutique also has an online shopping option, and I had shopped on its website eight or nine years ago when I was privately exploring my feminine self. Even when you are making an online purchase, staff are available for phone consultations, and they are always very discreet and helpful.

There are many other online-only shops worth looking into. A quick internet search can also help you locate local shops and multiple online options.

Stuart finds shopping easy

I agree with Aejaie that it's much easier for FTM trans people to shop for new clothes. In many cases, FTM trans people can live fairly androgynously or express their gender as outwardly male, and it's not considered unusual. For instance, Stuart Barette told me that there are online guides to assist with FTM transitions, including shopping and dressing. Among those are Hudson's FTM Resource Guide (www.ftmguide.org), a UK National Health Service-sponsored publication called *A Guide for Young Trans People in the UK* (http://cdn0.genderedintelligence.co.uk/2012/11/17/17-15-02-A-Guide-For-Young-People.pdf), and http://transitionftmuk.co.uk/appearance, which is a website created by a trans man in the UK who offers advice as a service to the community. These resources and numerous others provide helpful information for the transitioning FTM trans person, and the advice they provide is applicable anywhere, not just in the UK.

Behavior modifications for adapting to a new persona

Before I went back to work, my psychologist explained to me that it's not enough to look like a woman, dress and accessorize tastefully; you also need to learn how to gesture and speak in a more feminine way. The sound of your voice should be congruent and complementary to your appearance. I have found that it's just as important to change the way you behave as well as the way you dress in order to become more convincing and comfortable as the new you, and in so doing you will worry less about passing.

Gender-related speaking characteristics such as pitch, inflections, mannerisms, and conversational patterns can take years to be fully internalized, but the transitioning employee who suddenly changes to a new feminine gender expression has to adopt and exhibit them almost instantly in order to be congruent with her new appearance. Your voice conveys so much about you directly and indirectly. I spent a lot of time understanding how the typical male and female voices differ but making that conscious switch and establishing a "new normal" was extremely difficult for me, especially during the time before I completely transitioned to my female self.

My psychologist referred me to Maureen O'Connor, a local speech therapist who had been working with transgender patients for over 40 years. She put together a comprehensive treatment program that included exercises for adopting a new vocal pitch and melody, changing my resonance and voice quality, as well as word choice and non-verbal communication. Maureen works with many FTM trans people on dropping their pitch within the male range (now easy to determine with widely available tuning phone apps) and how to masculinize their resonance and other specific vocal behaviors like intonation, projection, and loudness. She also works with many MTF trans people to create an opposite set of skills—higher pitch and a softer speaking tone without resonance.

Maureen and I started working together almost immediately after I decided to transition. Our first diagnostic appointment lasted three hours and led to a rigorous training program that would teach me how to modulate my voice. For instance, I learned about the normal pitch ranges for cisgender male and female voices and how I could control my resonance—the "James Earl Jones effect" as Maureen put it. Pitch and resonance are the two critical factors which must change to achieve a feminine voice. Pitch is determined by the length, mass, thickness, size and tension of the vocal cords and measured in hertz: average=125 Hz for men, 200 Hz for women. Resonance is created as the sound is modified (damped and amplified), traveling up the vocal tract (pharynx, oral and nasal cavities) and out the mouth as speech.

I learned that I had a wide singing vocal range and that I could actually achieve a more feminine pitch which did not sound like falsetto but required effort and training. And I learned to modify both pitch (vocal cords) and resonance (vocal tract) simultaneously. During my sessions, (usually an hour every other week), I also practiced female melodic intonation patterns. Women usually express emotions with pitch changes; men more often use changes in loudness and speed. When we worked together, Maureen would model utterances for me to imitate. She also designed spontaneous speech practice without her model. Tasks were in a hierarchy of increasing length and difficulty. Self-listening and self-correction were stressed. She often re-directed me to my target pitch on a keyboard. Home practice and everyday use were assigned. We also practiced vocal "vegetative" behaviors: coughing, sneezing, throat clearing, and even laughing.

I would also read to Maureen and she would comment on the pitch and resonance of my voice as well as my behavior. She taught me other non-verbal gender patterns related to coughing, sneezing, throat clearing, and even laughing. Although I suppose I had been aware of these things, it was never as apparent as when it was pointed out and then I observed women afterwards.

Initially, I tried to achieve a certain target pitch, which was solidly in the feminine range. After a few months I could actually reach it regularly, but it did not seem to exude the same authority I wanted at work. I started to use a phone app that allowed me to determine the pitch of women who were speaking at the scientific meetings I attended for work. I noted that women who gave the most effective presentations generally used a slightly lower pitch that was different from what they would use conversationally. After experimenting with my voice at different pitches, I decided to target a pitch I could use in all scenarios that was in the lower end of the female range, because I felt it was more effective in the workplace and did not present too stark a difference from my original pitch. I have been pleased by how this has turned out for me and I have successfully reset what Maureen O'Connor referred to as my "internal voice." I very rarely catch myself at a lower pitch (usually when I am very tired or surprised), and when I recently saw Aejaie after almost a year, she thought I had done a good job to soften my voice without losing its presence and authority. I've also eliminated my resonance almost entirely. I still get mis-gendered occasionally over the phone, but I've come to terms with it—I accept it as a consequence of my decision to adopt more of a "work voice."

As part of my voice training, I also learned to identify and adopt gender conventions and speech patterns frequently used by women to maintain conversations. For example, women often follow a statement by "tagging" it with a question at the end, such as, "don't you agree?" or "wouldn't you say?" Men tend to make declarative statements, and then move on to the next topic.

I also worked with Aejaie at Carla's on other non-verbal aspects of my feminine persona, such as mastering a feminine style of walking (more of a glide) and adjusting my body language. I worked on sitting up straight, crossing my legs, and the way I folded my hands when seated at a table. Aejaie helped me to develop new habits related to feminine postures for sitting, standing and walking, and getting in out and of a car (who knew that men put one leg at a time in, while women typically sit first and swing both legs over?). Changing these ingrained habits can be difficult, depending on how old you are. Your automatic defaults need to be completely rewired, particularly how you interact with people when you're surprised or emotional. But, especially on my first day back, I was conscious of every move I made.

At the end of the first day back

My first day back to work was one of the most nerve-racking days of my life. I wore flared black linen slacks with a white button-down shirt with silver flowers printed across the chest, and some sensible low black pumps. Since I worked in the far corner of the building, I had a long walk down a hallway where many people in my team sat in offices or cubicles. The hallway seemed endless! But as I made my way toward my office, several people came out to greet me and made very supportive compliments, many saying I looked really great. My administrative assistant finally saw me and gave me a big hug and an approving smile. I'm not sure what they were expecting but I seemed to survive running that initial gauntlet pretty well.

The rest of the day was a whirlwind of similar encounters as more of my team got to see Dana for the first time. Once the buzz died down, I was able to settle back into my work and begin catching up from my extended absence. I couldn't stop thinking how happy and encouraged I was, and I was so pleased by the positive responses from nearly everyone. I got the feeling that I looked better than they had expected, which was a relief because I was so worried about how I was presenting as a woman. I tried hard not to appear too tentative, but in truth, I analyzed every conversation I had.

Each day became easier than the day before. After I made it through my first day, I decided that I would not initiate any further discussions about my transition, except when I encountered someone in the office who I had not spoken to personally about it. I would always respond to questions from anyone about my transition but usually in private conversations. I felt, however, that once I had announced my transition and come back to the office as the new me, I did not want to take people back to my prior life. The entire purpose of transition is to express your true gender identity and establish your authentic self in the workplace, so any revisiting or backtracking prevents the consolidation of your new persona in the eyes of others.

This didn't mean that I wasn't tempted to talk about my changes occasionally, even in self-deprecating ways. As I've said, people use the word "transition" in business parlance all the time, and I would occasionally think to myself, "That's a topic that I'm familiar with" or something similar. But I felt very strongly that it would diminish my efforts and keep reminding my co-workers of who I used to be, not who I now was, so I never said it out loud.

On one of my first days back, I did meet with a senior executive whom I had not spoken to personally about my change, but he had heard about it. As I approached him, I smiled and slightly spread my arms and called attention to the new me and said something awkward like, "Hi Rudi, it's the new me." He acknowledged my new look with a smile as I said I was sorry I hadn't had a chance to tell him in advance. I gave him a short version of my reasons to transition and he seemed very understanding. He remained very professional and collegial during all of our subsequent interactions.

Since then, there have been a handful of times when I've run into someone from my male past, and I've had to decide whether I wanted to disclose who I was when they didn't recognize me. I was recently on a business trip to London and I was out with some friends. It was World AIDS Day and we were attending a benefit at the National Theatre. There was a woman at the benefit who worked with my companions and had known me as a male. She approached my friends to say hello but didn't recognize me. Then my friend introduced me as Dana Pizzuti, and she looked at me for what seemed like a very long time and then had the "a-ha moment" when she realized that in fact she knew me as well. Once she realized who I was she was exuberant and said, "Oh my god, how are you? You look great. I have a trans daughter who's 28 years old and she's really struggling."

Also, as you spend more time at work after your transition, the normal employee turnover will work to your advantage. The proportion of people who knew you before the transition and had to make adjustments in their interactions with you afterwards will always be declining as people retire, resign, or transfer out and new co-workers are hired. Those new people who join the company will only know the new you, which is refreshing.

Have patience

It took me over a year until I was really comfortable in my office as Dana. One day I realized that I had stopped worrying so much about passing, my appearance, and how I sounded. It just took practice and getting used to it. Trust me, the new you will all come together but no matter where you are, you are a work in progress, just like everyone else. Be patient and try to be kind to yourself…you've gone through a lot!

Once you return to work, every day you should be putting in your best efforts to solidify your desired gender expression. The more you believe in yourself the better you will be able to be who you want to be, and over a short amount of time you will see that those around you will buy in. Just as with your medical treatments, you may feel as if you are in an enormous rush to achieve your final appearance. But you need to experiment and give yourself a chance to learn and adapt. You might not look exactly the way you envisioned or hoped, but the new you will eventually emerge and take hold. Do the best you can with what you have. You're going to continue to learn and adjust. I'm still a work in progress but am always incredibly happy that finally I am outwardly the woman I always was on the inside.

PART III

BEYOND THE REVEAL

CHAPTER 7

GETTING BACK TO WORK

It's impossible to know how long it will take for your company and co-workers to be completely comfortable with the new you, because there are several factors to evaluate. First, you have to know your corporate culture, and who you're working for in order to judge how it's going to go in the future. Are the majority of employees under 35? Is there a celebration of all types of diversity at your company? Are you in a creative field? Was there a clear pathway for your transition? If so, you are in luck—these are some of the best indicators that your transition will be easily accepted.

Our corporate culture did not celebrate diversity and was very goal-oriented. There was a pervasive fear of being chastised or criticized. I was in senior management, and I was always judged by the success of my team's performance on our last project. The underlying cultural messages were, "What have you done for us lately? You're only valuable if you do what you're told, don't cause problems, and prevent future problems. And, most importantly, don't make waves!"

It was an exhilarating place to work when all was going well, but it also could be a vindictive, demeaning, and stressful environment. Yet at the same time the unspoken corporate culture demanded that you were not supposed to be too aggressive. There was a clear patriarchy, and even in senior management we felt that we were only supposed to speak when spoken to. And that was true from the day I got there, eight years before I announced that I was going to transition. All of these factors made my transition challenging. However, I was able to deal with them, and stay in my job until I was ready to leave.

No matter what type of company you work for, and what the corporate culture is like, you bear a great deal of the responsibility for the success of your transition in terms of how you are accepted back into the workplace. We should assume that most companies in LGBTQ+-friendly states (see Chapter 3) really do want to help you have a successful transition, not only for altruistic reasons, but to retain you as a valuable employee. Furthermore, when companies can ensure you will be supported and not harassed or otherwise discriminated against, they are limiting their exposure to potential legal action.

However, it would be unrealistic to expect that there are no real pitfalls to being transgender in the workplace. Data from Out Now's *Show Me The Business Case* reveals that transgender employees have a more difficult time in the workforce than others. Many transgender workers report that they feel as if they are being judged differently from other cisgender employees. It is extremely hard to identify whether an unconscious bias exists against trans people in any company, and many transgender workers believe that they have become marginalized within their organization. Subtle slights occur, such as if you are no longer included in meetings that you had routinely attended, or if you are not invited to events outside the office. More overt snubs could include being passed over for a promotion or high-profile projects. In many cases, you may not even be aware that you have been excluded from a meeting or from consideration for a project unless you have a friend, an ally, or other source of intelligence who will keep you informed.

The goal of this chapter is to expose these pitfalls so that you can anticipate, avoid, or create a game plan for dealing with them and come out ahead. The ultimate goal is for you to keep your career moving forward at your company in the short term, and to enhance your earning potential and job satisfaction in the long term.

YOU ARE NOT ALONE

One of the things I was most worried about when I returned to work was feeling isolated, and that experience was one of my primary motivations for writing this book. It's easy to find yourself feeling alone and believe that you are the only one who has gone through such an important transition. With the help of my support group and good friends, I was better able to navigate.

Later, I realized that there was a whole world of transgender people waiting to help me that I wished I had been able to access during my most challenging moments. Time after time, I have felt strong support from the LGBTQ+ community. So remember, besides this book, there are many online resources available for nearly every aspect of your transition. One of my favorites for providing information is Out & Equal, an LGBTQ+ workplace advocacy organization. You are never alone!

Pitfall 1: The career stall
The fix: Keep your career moving forward

I've heard of too many examples of trans people who remain with their employer after their transition yet find that their career development stalls. While any withdrawal of support can be subtle, it can also be devastating if you had been a high performer or praised as an asset to your organization prior to your initial declaration. The career development you may have received before the transition frequently ends, and career progression can be slowed or completely stalled deliberately without violating workplace discrimination rules.

The stories I've heard usually go something like this: the transition is initially successful. HR is on board and is legally doing all the right things. Yet a few months later, from a career development point of view, you begin to feel stuck. For instance, one transgender woman I met at a workplace advocacy conference, works at a Fortune 500 company was a highly regarded in-house writer. When she first announced her transition, both the company and her boss were very supportive. But when an internal opening for a new position was posted, which would have been a promotion for her, even though her boss recommended her for the job, she was told she was not a candidate for it because her boss's boss was not supportive, effectively blocking her opportunity to advance. And although it wasn't explicitly stated that she was denied the promotion because she was trans, she had never felt accepted and understood by the supervisor. She now believes that her potential is perceived differently within her organization despite strong support from her boss, and she's very disappointed about that. Yet she decided to remain with the company because she loved her job, needed the income, and wasn't ready to give up the retirement plan and pension she has worked so hard to qualify for. At first this transwoman felt stifled, but after several months she found a new position at a higher level at the same company. Sometimes, it just takes time to find the right fit and to get your career trajectory back on track.

While it may seem obvious, the best way to keep your career moving forward is to be a model employee in the job you have right now. Try not to let your transition-related concerns distract you from showing up day after day with a confident, positive attitude, and meet all your deadlines with the highest quality output. Treat your job the same way you did before; in effect, as if you never transitioned. Try to be the same high-performing person you always were.

Once you stop worrying about your physical appearance and what your co-workers may be thinking, you can let your work take center stage. I'm not saying that these suggestions will come easily—you will have to be mindful and alert to resist distractions that can inhibit your self-confidence and momentum toward your goals—but they are the key to success. Here are some tips to keep you on track.

Be resolute

Exude absolute confidence in your ability to do your work. You have done the right thing by transitioning, and both you and your company are better off when you are comfortably operating as your authentic self. Data from Out Now, *Show Me The Business Case* shows that employee turnover is significantly lower if transgender employees feel comfortable being out to their co-workers, and it is expected that employees who are out will be more productive for the business. Even though you have changed your appearance, you belong at the company and there should be no question that you can pick up just where you left off and continue doing the same great work. Don't shy away from having hard discussions with your manager about your career development and competencies necessary to make it to the next level. You may have to remind your boss through your work that you're the same excellent employee you've always been, and you're entitled to have the same degree of career development. Go the extra mile by showing that you are committed to the company. Volunteer for extra projects if available, and take on opportunities within the organization that could help the company as well as your own career advancement.

When I came back to the office, I never worried about how well I was doing my job. I liked my job and was good at it; I had built a large, high-performing team of 400+ people over the previous eight years and I knew how I needed to lead them, and what I needed to do to make them successful. And we always met our goals! So there was no lack of confidence in my leadership ability, which was also reinforced by all the positive emails I received before I left for my first surgery.

Like the way you look

Try not to be tentative about your new gender. At first, I had very little confidence about my gender expression, and that may have affected how others perceived my performance at work. I was overly worried about passing: I wondered what other people thought about my appearance, and if I was acting feminine enough. I was also unsure about how to act as a woman at my level in that office. In reality, my new persona was more of a true reflection of who I was on the inside, so I shouldn't have been so reluctant expressing it. Even if you're unsure of the way you look, try not to show it. Take to heart any compliments you receive; other people's positive feedback will be a reminder that you're presenting well even when you are feeling unsure. Your confidence will bring others along and will eventually change your own perception of yourself. They say "fake it till you make it" for a reason.

Body language is very important in how we are perceived by others, so be mindful of your posture and of making eye contact during one-on-one interactions or in a meeting. I found that just sitting up straight and leaning forward in meetings really helped me to be engaged and keep interpersonal connections. It also signaled that I was a confident woman.

Amy Cuddy, PhD, who teaches at Harvard Business School, has spoken extensively and done provocative but controversial research on the effects of "power posing," which refers to adopting open and assertive postures as a technique for improving performance in business and other settings. She has concluded that even temporarily adopting positive body language helps others and the individual feel more confident and perceived as successful in social settings. Although some of the concerns about her research center around the effect of power posing on hormone levels, she has examined its effect on other psychological outcomes. In a 2016 article about her work by Jesse Singal and Melissa Dahl that appeared in *The Cut*, Cuddy states:

> My lab recently conducted a systematic review and statistical analysis of power posing studies. It shows strong and robust evidence that adopting expansive postures does indeed increase feelings of power. ... In addition, many studies have shown that adopting expansive postures increases happiness, mood, and other related emotion variables.[1]

The same article in *The Cut* referred to a review by Adam Galinsky and co-workers at Columbia University who concluded that the "sense of power...produces a range of cognitive, behavioral, and physiological consequences, including improved executive functioning, general optimism, creativity, authenticity, the ability to self-regulate, and performance in various domains, to name a handful." In one sense, you can pretend to be confident by adopting these poses, which may actually help you feel better and be more confident!

Compartmentalize your life

Undoubtedly, you will be going through many physical and emotional changes and potential turmoil in multiple aspects of your life that will coincide with the change of your gender expression at work. Many trans people find their home life is just as chaotic as work. On top of that, you may be caught up in your schedule of medical appointments and surgeries, or the recoveries, that have to take place during work hours. However, it is very important to try to keep each of these areas of your life distinct; otherwise, your home life and medical schedule can create huge distractions in the workplace. Even though there will be personal aspects that play out between you and your co-workers, it is important to maintain your focus on

---

1   www.thecut.com/2016/09/read-amy-cuddys-response-to-power-posing-critiques.
    html.

the job. For me, I was relieved to put aside my most personal issues surrounding my home life and how I was actually feeling during the work day and immerse myself in my job.

Gather intelligence

Do not trust that your work life will "go back to normal" because you believe in the company and it is saying the right things about diversity and inclusion. I naively assumed that once I got through the transition I would be treated like everyone else. Before my transition, I had received several awards that were tagged to my performance, including financial incentives like extra stock. Afterwards, these perks stopped, and within a few months following my transition I realized that I was only being asked to represent the company outside the office on LGBTQ+ issues. While I was happy to do this work, at the same time it was stifling my growth as a leader in other areas. I began to believe that I wasn't going to get any further in the company. And it became very clear, once I no longer was given opportunities to represent the company in ways I had previously been asked to, that my boss no longer recognized my value and experience, and no longer supported me.

It is important to try to establish some back channels or reliable sources (friends or supportive co-workers) within the company who have insight into what is going on within the leadership of the company and to see if there have been instances of exclusion or marginalizing. If they occur, don't hesitate to discuss with your manager or HR to find out the rationale and express your interest in volunteering for projects and regaining any lost ground.

Seek help

Connect with management and other internal resources who can help you advance your career. Start with human resources. Explore the diversity group, if your company has one, or other allies in your office, as discussed in Chapter 4 and Chapter 8. Network with other LGBTQ+ organizations to create external support, like Out & Equal in the US, OUTstanding in the UK, or the National Center for Transgender Equality, an advocacy and lobbying group in Washington, DC.

Pitfall 2: Feeling like a marginalized employee
The fix: Check your old privilege

In the office, it's safe to assume you will now be judged in many different ways. For me, this meant that I was now evaluated as a woman, a transgender person, and in comparison to my prior self. My company, like most, had a very white, male, heterosexual power structure. When I think more carefully about the demographics of my company at the time, there were very few women at my level. Of all executive management, including vice presidents and above, no more than 20 percent were women. To me, this meant that the company had a problem with gender to begin with. Not transgender, just gender.

I quickly learned that I was not going to be treated the way I had been when I was David; I no longer had the same male privilege. As a male, there are well-recognized advantages and allowances for behaviors that are less favored in women, such as aggression, assertiveness, and even dominance. Although it is beyond the scope of this book to dissect the details and implications of gender in the workplace, a certain awareness of this reality is important, as a MTF trans person gives up her male privilege and assumes a female gender role at work. And while I don't feel that women need to behave like men to succeed, they need to adjust and be able to hold their ground within workplace norms, which can vary by the business, the geography, and the company culture. An excellent summary of the differences among the genders in the workplace can be found in *Communicate with Confidence: How to Say it Right the First Time and Every Time*, by Dianna Booher, a communication consultant and best-selling author. In her chapter on gender differences, she states that to a certain extent, the difference in gender communication can be attributed to the power dynamic, so that when women obtain more power they will communicate differently. She writes:

> As women grow up in our culture they are taught not to be confrontational—not to make a scene or be aggressive or pushy…[while] women have become more assertive in their language, they still struggle against the label and perception of aggressiveness. They still want to be considered "nice." So how do they express opposition to an idea? Often they use questions to redirect someone's thinking. They also, of course, use questions in the traditional way—to solicit information, to build consensus around an idea, or to develop their staff members and help them rethink their positions, plans, or ideas.[2]

Aejaie taught me that I had to relearn how to "work a room." She said, "If you're a male leader and you have three alpha males who work for you it's one thing, but when you transition and you're still their boss, you have to relearn how to control a meeting and manage your three alpha males." There would be a different dynamic in play, so I needed to work doubly hard to maintain my leadership but in a less confrontational way. It is not fair but, unfortunately, trans women may have to work harder to manage their teams afterward, but your talent and leadership abilities and instincts will still be there for you to draw on.

The loss of my male privilege became particularly clear during meetings. No matter how prepared I thought I was before coming back to work, I wasn't ready for the difficulty of interacting as a woman in meetings, where it was harder to break into the conversation in a less aggressive mode and with a softer voice, especially on conference calls. And to have to put up with that, while knowing that all it would take was for me to be really aggressive,

---

2   Booher, D. (2011) *Communicate with Confidence: How to Say it Right the First Time and Every Time.* New York, NY: McGraw-Hill Education, pp.375–376.

like a man would react, but in a way that would be seen as a major faux pas from a woman, made it that much harder. Most men don't realize how poorly women are treated in the workplace. Yet after a transition, trans women are treated just as badly as women have always been treated. It's a big "a-ha" moment about the truth of corporate America once you voluntarily relinquish your male privilege. But MTF trans people like me have had the experience of being male so we can draw on that strength and knowledge occasionally when we need to assert ourselves, even if we have now to do it in a completely different, gender-appropriate way.

Another example of male privilege is the fact that one of the important characteristics valued in management is known as "executive presence." This refers directly to whether you are perceived to be in command and confident in your role—in other words, how quick on your feet, confident and self-assured you are. It is a very subjective concept, yet at the same time it is a trait that recruiters and managers look for in potential leaders. How was I supposed now to project the same executive presence as a woman? I noticed that the men in my office frequently held their bodies in a powerful stance or position in meetings, leaning back and taking up space.

Ultimately, I tried to take gender out of my work as much as possible. This doesn't mean I dressed or acted androgynously; it means I tried to do the best possible job and not adopt overly masculine or feminine traits. I compromised some of my aspirations for how I wanted Dana to appear at work but supplemented my new persona with some effective tactics I had used as a male.

If you work in a more female-dominated industry, it is very possible that you will not have as difficult a time fitting in and asserting yourself. But if you're reporting to work as a woman at a typical job, and you see clearly that you are not operating within a level playing field with the men or other cisgender employees, resign yourself to the fact that you will have to work harder to prove yourself and get ahead.

Finally, do not be afraid to advocate for yourself if you think you are experiencing gender bias. These days, there is a heightened awareness of harassment and discrimination on the basis of gender, so point it out when you see it. Now, more than ever, people are listening.

Morgan's FTM experience at work

Some FTM transgender people may feel that they have acquired male privilege. Some trans men have told me that they experienced less discrimination or harassment after their transitions than they did as lesbian women previously.

Morgan had transitioned when he was working at a small art dealer. Soon after, he had an opportunity to apply for a position at a prominent auction house in New York City. His recruitment experience went smoothly but he still had one challenge with his appearance. He told me the following story:

> I was very comfortable in my old job with a smaller art dealer where I had transitioned, but then a new position opened up at one of the premier auction houses in the world. I had a friend who worked there and he thought I would be a good fit for this position and offered to be a reference for me. I went through the interview process and landed the job. I felt right away that people there could see me as a talented individual; they were not too concerned whether I was male or female, but cared that I was a competent and trustworthy employee.
>
> When you work in the arts, you're used to a slightly different crowd than say if you were a lawyer or a doctor. It's just one of those things that it's less entrenched in a "traditional" lifestyle or a "traditional" way of outward appearance. People don't really bat an eye when it comes to various means of self-expression. This is such a progressive company; I have colleagues with tattoos and facial piercings. But when I started my new job, and some people at the firm knew I was transgender, the only problem

Human Resources seemed to have was with my earrings. My manager was concerned that their clients would not be okay with the little gauges I was wearing. The conflict with this problem was that if the earrings were removed, they left a noticeable hole that I couldn't change or undo. After informing them of this fact, they backed off and the earrings became a non-issue relatively quickly. Since then, a few clients have made comments about the gauges, but I make it clear that they are simply a part of who I am and do not affect my ability to do my job.

Ultimately, the clients realize that my earrings might be weird, but I'm also really good at my job. If you don't want to work with me, that's fine. There are plenty of other people you can work with, but they might not be able to help you the way I can. It's their decision. I just leave it up to them. I'm not uncomfortable with it, why should someone else be?

Did his newly found male privilege come into play in regard to ending the conversation about the earrings? It's hard to tell. I was called out for specifically the same issue, but the only difference was that I was looking more feminine, and Morgan was looking more masculine.

Pitfall 3: Being treated like a curiosity
The fix: Focus on your pioneer
spirit and exceptional skills

It's hard to put aside everything that you have been going through and to take your co-worker's perspective. However, for the majority of cisgender employees, having anyone in the office change their gender expression is still regarded as a new phenomenon. It is very likely that you may be the first trans person they have ever met. In the past and in other cultures, the majority of transgender people were not even considered for mainstream employment and ended up in entertainment, the sex trade, very menial jobs or focusing their careers in areas that service or support other transgender people. Now that we are living in more enlightened times and in a more progressive environment (at least in some parts of the country) I consider us fortunate. There are dozens of forward-thinking companies who embrace and actively recruit members of the LGBTQ+ community, and I recognize that we are still a very small fraction of all potential employees.

Our job then, whether we like it or not, is to be the best we can be, understand where our co-workers are coming from and their overall unfamiliarity with our community, just as we are asking them to understand our perspective, and show them what we can do. We are pioneers of the workforce. It may be an extra burden, but we are up to it!

I have heard it said that Barack Obama carried an extra burden as the first African-American president, and felt he had to be doubly impeccable to set an example for all people about how well a black man could do his job. And it showed! Near the end of his presidency, an article in the *Huffington Post* blog by Cody Cain entitled *Obama has outclassed the grand old white establishment*, summarized his performance in office despite the vigorous attacks and concerted opposition to him and his policies:

> Being the first black President of the United States is a daunting undertaking. Occupying the White House for anyone is like living in a public fish bowl, but for the first black president, everything is magnified a thousand times... Throughout it all, President Obama has been a model of dignity, grace, and elegance. Even under the bright lights of such intense public scrutiny and in the face of such despicable personal attacks, he has always maintained his composure. Cool as a cucumber. He has consistently risen above the pettiness of those attacking him and demonstrated the true qualities of honor and respectability.[3]

Sound familiar? We are held to a higher standard. And we can meet it.

---

3   www.huffingtonpost.com/cody-cain/first-black-president-out_b_7896968.html.

In my conversations with other trans people who supported me as I planned my transition at work, and as part of the research for this book, I came to an interesting realization about trans people as employees. Most trans people who have decided to transition share several characteristics which are valued in the workplace. Most notable are:

- the capacity to self-reflect and understand who they are and how they need to exist in the world

- the capability to analyze many aspects of a complex and difficult decision (such as coming out and transitioning in the workplace)

- the courage to be vulnerable to others in disclosing a deep truth

- a willingness to take risks

- the ability to consider and accept the consequences of an important decision.

The fact that you have decided to transition in itself is admirable and should be applauded by companies who want employees who are brave, thoughtful, and comfortable in their own skin. You are already exceptional; don't let anyone tell you otherwise.

CHAPTER 8

CREATING A SUPPORT SYSTEM FOR THE WORKPLACE

In the first few months following your transition to your preferred gender expression, you'll need all the friends you can muster. This is particularly true at work, where you'll be spending the majority of your time. I've found that the more open and honest you are about your transition, the easier it will be to bring others on board, to support you during difficult times, and celebrate your good days.

While the strong personal relationships that you've formed on your own will be your primary support, today's more progressive companies are creating formalized support networks. They are often referred to as *ally programs*. Allies can be an individual or group of individuals that are associated with one another to support a common cause or purpose. An ally in the context of LGBTQ+ inclusion policies in the workplace refers to those people who choose to support LGBTQ+ colleagues. According to the HRC, allies can be non-LGBTQ+ individuals as well as those within the LGBTQ+ community who support each other. For instance, a gay man can be an ally to someone who is gender fluid. In many companies, most allies are non-LGBTQ+ colleagues, and the list of ally initiatives for various groups in the workplace is growing, whether it is for LGBTQ+, women, or racial minorities.

In 2016, Out Now Global surveyed 2584 individuals in a targeted ally survey in 60 countries. It revealed that 57 percent of respondents were heterosexual, 31 percent were lesbian or gay, 6 percent were bisexual and 6 percent were transgender. The survey stated the importance of non-LGBT+ allies:

> There is a strongly held view among most respondents that stated visible support from management is key to making it easier for people to become Allies at work. Out Now's experience has been that the higher the management support given to support LGBT people, the more effective the inclusion outcomes achieved… Workplace culture is an odd concept insofar as it actually happens on a day-to-day basis "when nobody is looking" yet the workplace tone that informs prevailing culture, particularly in relation to LGBT inclusion, is very much set from the top… Failure to provide leadership to teams is one of the most frequently cited issues Allies reported, making their endeavours less successful. Conversely, in enterprises where management is clear that LGBT inclusion is a corporate asset, respondents generally report higher levels of support and results for their efforts.[1]

The reason ally networks are important is simple—they work. Allies are meant to offer support to the individual, but also to advocate and defend them when they are not present, especially in instances of discrimination, ridicule, and harassment. According to a 2013 survey by the Center for Talent Innovation, nearly a quarter of LGBT+ workers who responded said that having a strong network of allies at work convinced them to come out. Being a trans-inclusive ally can be particularly meaningful.[2]

---

1   www.outnowconsulting.com/media/25552/Report-Allies-2016-V11.pdf.
2   https://qz.com/926596/how-to-make-your-office-welcoming-to-transgender-and-gender-non-conforming-workers.

In light of the #MeToo and #TimesUp movements, having allies for women in the workplace has never been more important. The same holds true for the LGBTQ+ community. In the business world, there is an extremely positive reaction from the LGBTQ+ community to anyone in senior management who is either out or a strong and visible ally for the community. The Out Now survey showed that an important factor affecting whether people choose to support LGBT+ colleagues is whether there is stated and visible support by management for doing so (cited as "very important" by 63% of respondents).

For instance, as far back as 2011, Stonewall UK, an LGBT+ rights and advocacy organization, completed a report with Goldman Sachs entitled *Straight Allies: How they Help Create Gay-Friendly Workplaces,* which acknowledge the strong desire on the part of heterosexuals to support legal protection for sexual orientation in the workplace.

There were two notable quotes from that report that are still relevant today:[3]

"Straight allies, particularly at senior levels, are fundamental to making gay equality work because if you're seen to be the gay member of staff who's running around doing it on your own then people think 'all the work you're doing is self-serving, you're only helping yourself, you're helping a small group.' So I think there's a huge role for straight allies because they lend credibility, they help unlock resources, they get buy-in internally and they impress people externally. If you don't have the support of straight allies then people will always ask 'why are you doing this? Isn't this favouritism? Why are you just catering to a certain group?'" (Daniel Winterfeldt, Head of International Capital Markets, CMS Cameron McKenna LLP)

"The [Goldman Sachs] Managing Director Ally programme is about getting the broadest, most representative group of senior

---

3   www.stonewall.org.uk/sites/default/files/straight_allies.pdf.

people involved in LGBT issues, acting as informed advocates, sitting in senior positions in all the divisions. The leveraging effect of that is significant, because you've got a lot of people talking about the issues, using the [same] words and talking to other colleagues. And people look upwards to see what their managers are doing. They see what they're saying. They see that they're proud to be associated with the programme. They see what actions they're taking... I think senior people have a critical role in setting the tone because people look to the leadership to understand what's important to the organisation. They look at what leaders say and do. And here at Goldman Sachs the championing of diversity comes from the very top and that's why people see that it's very important to us." (Glenn Earle, Chief Operating Officer of European Businesses, Goldman Sachs)

In June 2017, I attended a breakfast sponsored by OUTstanding and hosted by LinkedIn in San Francisco, where two companies disclosed their efforts to improve "allyship." Bank of America, which currently employs approximately 200,000 individuals and is based in Charlotte, North Carolina, had begun an effort to enlist 25,000 allies across its businesses, especially in senior management. At the time of the meeting, it had already exceeded 20,000 identified allies. SAP, a software company employing over 88,000 employees and based in Germany, has specific inclusion and diversity goals for all senior executives. Its executives' compensation is partly based on their visible participation as allies and whether their segments of the business recruit and hire a diverse workforce.

I recently heard a story about the importance of a single ally gesture that was broadcast on a webinar sponsored by Out & Equal. Cheryl Gilliam, a senior packaging engineer from Kellogg's, based in Battle Creek, Michigan, told how in 2016 they were organizing the first Pride parade in Battle Creek. Another Kellogg's executive, Norma Barnes Eureste, Vice President and Chief Counsel, was the marshall for the parade. Both women were thrilled to see the President of Kellogg's entire North American Operations, Paul Norman, turn up and stay to watch the entire event. The fact that he attended made a lasting impression on the Kellogg LGBTQ+ employees as well as the onlookers. These examples of senior leadership showing up to support the LGBTQ+ community are critical to acceptance and the recruitment of other allies to champion diversity and inclusion.

The UK's *Financial Times* publishes an annual list of leading LGBT allies compiled and reviewed by OUTstanding. Among the leading LGBT+ allies in 2017 were Denise Morrison, President and CEO of Campbell Soup Company (number 1), Paul Polman, CEO of Unilever (number 3), and Mark Zuckerberg, Founder and CEO of Facebook (number 7).

How do allies help?

The 2016 Out Now ally survey found that the most common action undertaken by LGBT+ allies was to mention LGBT+ people or topics positively in the workplace, which was done by 87 percent of respondents. The second most common action was speaking up against an anti-LGBT+ discussion others were having at work (43%). Allies can challenge and address any inappropriate banter and discussions they hear, and explain relevant terminology (transgender as opposed to transsexual, for example). Sometimes, information from an ally has more authority than a comment from someone directly involved.

On its website, Straight for Equality lists ten things effective allies can accomplish:[4]

1. Become informed about the realities, challenges, and issues affecting the lives of LGBT+ people through websites, books, documentaries, and educational materials.

2. Be open about having gay friends, family, or acquaintances that you value, respect, and are grateful to have in your life.

---

4   www.straightforequality.org.

When you talk about them, don't omit the fact that they're LGBT+.

3. Speak up when you hear derogatory slurs or jokes and don't tell them yourself.

4. Ask if you are unsure how an LGBT+ friend, family member, or acquaintance would like their significant other to be referred to or introduced, rather than avoiding acknowledgment of the relationship.

5. Help your kids learn about and appreciate different kinds of families. Be mindful of the day-to-day messages that they are receiving about gay and transgender people and issues in school, from friends, and on TV. Talk about these with them.

6. Quit or don't join organizations that overtly discriminate. Let them know why you are leaving, or not joining in the first place.

7. Support LGBT+-owned and LGBT+-friendly businesses, as well as ally businesses that have policies in place to ensure equal treatment for all.

8. Educate your place of worship on which organizations are inclusive, and which ones aren't.

9. Write letters to the editor of your newspaper to comment as a straight ally on why you support respectful and equal treatment for LGBT+ people.

10. Call, write, email, or visit public policy makers and let them know that as a straight person who votes, you support laws that extend equal rights and protections to all people.

For the transgender community, the importance of allies inside and outside work cannot be underestimated. Even in the most progressive of places, our safety is a paramount concern. And even on a personal level, there will be days when the enormity of your experience may be too much to bear. For example, I was once having a really hard day at work in my old company. I found myself talking very openly to a close friend named Korab, who I met in the LGBTQ+ support group at my company. I didn't really know Korab before we formed the support group, and now that I know him, I have great respect for him. He's an activist from Kosovo who was granted asylum in the US because he was gay. At the time, I was about two years post-transitioning, and I was telling him that I was having a hard time with my boss, who had given me some unfavorable feedback with little tangible evidence to support his claim that I was disengaged. Korab looked at me and said, "Dana, look at all that you've done, not only here, but in your career. Why do you care so much about these trivial comments? Don't worry so much about it. You're such an inspiration for everybody, not just the LGBT people in the company, so just keep doing what you're doing and be yourself."

His comments made a world of difference to me. In fact, they allayed my fears and reinforced that I was a dedicated employee who was setting a good example and trying to do the right thing. Korab helped me see that I was still a good executive; I knew what I was doing, and I knew how to run my team. Without his kindness I would probably still be questioning my leadership abilities and would be less aware of the positive impact my transition has had on other employees.

Recruiting your allies

You will want to develop your own allies in your organization. Not only will they be your friends, allies should be comfortable enough with you to give you a heads-up if there are issues related to your transition that have impacted what others think and say about you when you are not present. It is to be hoped that these people will be honest with you, so that you can craft a plan to deal effectively with office gossip or worse.

I periodically asked people I trusted and who had some insight into what was happening in senior leadership across the organization, "Have you heard anything negative related to my transition? Have people been talking about it?" I wanted to be aware if there was an issue I had created or may have overlooked which could impact me or the success of my team. Although I checked in with several people, they never mentioned hearing any negativity and I trusted that they would have felt comfortable telling me. Having this feedback was enough for me to feel that as far as my outward communication and activities were going, there was no trouble brewing.

If you have a solid and positive relationship with your manager, and he or she is supportive of you, there is no reason they cannot be an ally. Aejaie Sellers taught me that the best-case scenario when transitioning on the job is when you can set up a monthly or quarterly meeting with your manager, and use that time to check in. You can answer questions or address concerns that might have come up since your initial declaration. You can also inform them as to where you are in your transition in terms of medical treatments or procedures, your physical recovery, and how things are going at home. Knowing this information will help them better manage your workload, and your overall performance. Unfortunately, in my case, my manager wasn't particularly interested in any of the details or personal aspects of my transition except to the extent that I would be out of the office. He was tolerant but not particularly supportive.

If you don't or can't have an ally relationship with your boss or manager, see if you can recruit someone in your HR department, or better yet the diversity and inclusion group, if your company has one. First, they may be able to teach you how to explain to your boss how important it is for them to be more empathetic in general, and to you specifically. There will be special considerations you might need to address. For instance, if you are coming back from GRS, you may not be comfortable sitting for long periods of time, even after your "official" recovery period. Depending on your particular situation and the procedure you may have had, you may have difficulty walking long distances, or may need a place to do the required aftercare or build back your stamina for making it through the work day. At a minimum, HR should have an informed knowledge of what's going on with a transitioning employee mentally and physically, as opposed to just understanding the legal issues surrounding your transition.

Meet Tiffany, ally to doctors and nurses, students and teachers

Tiffany works for the diversity affairs office at a major academic medical center in New York City, which not only supports the doctors and hospital staff, but medical and nursing students. In that capacity, she is the go-to person for all LGBTQ+ employees and students. She has found that for LGBTQ+ students at the medical school, one of the hardest things they face is being in a traditionally conservative environment that doesn't really relate to who they are. She told me that there have been a few students she has met who are out as either trans, gender fluid, or non-binary. She talks with these students regularly, almost as a mentor, about what they're going to wear and how they're going to express themselves in their clerkship year, where they are evaluated by more traditional senior medical staff, nurses, and patients. As she said, "I always tell students that they get to make the decision; it's really up to them. We talk about the pros and cons, like if you wear makeup but predominantly appear masculine, that's something that I support and technically our policy supports, but it does not mean that there will not be bias in the subjective grades they're given by random attending physicians who are working with them."

She has also seen incidences of trans patients (and students) being treated poorly and has advocated on their behalf as well. Her hope is that holding senior staff accountable is the best way to enact that change. She told me, "If the people at the top don't really understand what they're doing regarding the professional and respectful treatment of all patients, they can talk the talk all they want, but they are not actually walking the walk. There are other healthcare companies that do walk the walk and I'm finding them and connecting our staff to learning opportunities. It's important that we not only tolerate diversity, but support and actually encourage diversity."

Cultivate allies by joining an employee resource group

You can begin to cultivate your own circle of allies in your workplace by identifying and connecting with other LGBTQ+ employees. As I've said before, I've found this larger community to be among the most supportive. You can find them through formal workplace clubs, support groups in or out of the workplace, or even lunch groups. In the workplace, the fastest way to do this is to join an LGBTQ+ ERG (employee resource group).

ERGs are quite common in larger companies. They are formalized employee groups formed around a specific population—women, African-Americans, Latinos, veterans, and often LGBTQ+ employees. They are meant to create community within the larger organization, and foster relationships that go beyond the workplace. They are often sponsored by the HR department. An ERG operates within a budget, which it can use in different ways, depending on the nature of the group. The members of the ERG set their own agenda based on what they think are the most important aspects of the workplace that need to be addressed. The group can be social, political, or somewhere in between. An HR employee may be assigned to each ERG, which may also have another sponsor, usually an executive within the company. As a vice president, I was part of the steering committee for the LGBTQ+ ERG, and I was also part of the women's group.

There was no LGBTQ+ support community for me to join when I transitioned. Then about nine months later, someone started a Facebook group to get employees together to participate in the

San Francisco Gay Pride Parade. I joined immediately. It grew from there, and I became part of the planning committee for the 2016 parade. That was the first time that the company had ever participated in the San Francisco Pride Parade, which is mind boggling since the company had been around for 30 years and nearly all the large and small technology and pharmaceutical companies (and pretty much every other business and government office) in the Bay Area participated. Over time, the ERG grew and we participated in major conferences, and even put on social events like movie screenings.

As your ERG grows there will naturally be more allies who are supportive of your transition. It is critical to try to personally get to know as many of them as you can, since there is no such thing as too much support. Usually the ERG will have an executive sponsor for a high level of senior leadership.

The company where I work now, Rigel is much smaller, but there are many LGBTQ+ employees who work and socialize together. There is less of a need for a formal ERG, but I feel well supported with lots of allies. The CEO, Raul Rodriguez, is gay, and he sets a positive tone for diversity and inclusion in the company.

SPOTLIGHT ON CIGNA

Dr. Renee McLaughlin, a transgender physician who works at Cigna's corporate office, is a member of its LGBT+ ERG, which is referred to as a colleague resource group. There is also a separate transgender advisory subcommittee within the group. Renee believes that of the more than 37,000 employees at Cigna, there are over 300 members of its LGBT+ ERG nationwide, which includes both LGBT+ employees and allies. Each colleague resource group is managed through the HR department as part of its diversity and inclusion organization.

Create your own ERG—spotlight on Credit Suisse

If your workplace does not have an ERG dedicated to the LGBTQ+ community, consider working with your HR department to initiate one. See how much of a difference you can make just by being active. For instance, Pips Bunce identifies as gender fluid and non-binary and is a director at Credit Suisse in the UK. She made her initial declaration at the same time she helped launch the company's LGBTQ+ ally program, for which she is the co-leader. Today, there are thousands of allies within the organization. The organization has created internal videos and guidebooks about trans inclusion, supports dual image pass cards for gender fluid employees, and has pioneered many other initiatives to support the trans community within the workplace. She reported to me that she's happy to work in an environment that is literally covered in LGBTQ+ ally stickers; she feels completely included and knows that when she is at work people have her back regardless of how she chooses to express, as some days Pips expresses in female form and other days as male.

Where else can you find allies?

If you are the only LGBTQ+ employee and you are having difficulty forming alliances, you can still count on the internet for creating community. There are many national and international LGBTQ+ organizations where you can find support and build alliances. These organizations provide LGBTQ+ networks as well as resources for starting your own networks more locally.

- Out & Equal Workplace Advocates: according to its website, this is the world's premier non-profit organization dedicated to achieving LGBTQ+ workplace equality. Its mandate is to partner with leading large companies and government agencies to provide leadership development, training, and networking opportunities that are meant to build inclusive and welcoming work environments. It hosts national and regional events throughout the year.

- OUTstanding: this British organization has a unique mission—to harness LGBTQ+ talent, among other diversity categories, to foster inclusive cultures in the workplace. It holds networking events where everyone is welcome, from senior executives to individual contributors.

- Human Rights Campaign (HRC): this non-profit organization represents more than three million members nationwide. It is the largest national LGBTQ+ civil rights organization whose mission is to ensure basic equal rights in order to create a safe environment at home and at work for its community. It produces a newsletter and blog to keep members abreast of local and national news of interest to the community.

- PFLAG (formerly known as Parents, Friends (& Family) of Lesbians and Gays): this non-profit organization is made up of LGBT+ individuals, family members, and other allies, and is known as the extended family of the LGBT+ community. Its primary mission is to support and advocate for community members. Today there are more than 400 PFLAG chapters across the US. If there is not a chapter in your community, the national organization is available for providing the support you may need.

- Straight for Equality: this organization is the national outreach and education program started by PFLAG specifically to support allies. It is an excellent resource for family members, or for HR to create connections for learning opportunities and advocacy. It offers online tools and resources.

- National Center for Transgender Equality (NCTE): this is the leading social justice advocacy organization for transgender people in the US. Aside from its Legal Services Network, it runs various projects to empower transgender people and their allies in and out of the workplace. It offers forums through its Voices of Trans Equality initiative to enable community members to connect directly and receive resources. It also runs ally-only programs for family members at no cost to participants.

Be someone else's ally

Among the most important actions that an ally can take is to spot and if possible prevent or advocate against harassment or discrimination in the workplace. There are different strategies around how to intervene in a harassment or discrimination situation, depending on whether you can or can't directly confront the person who is doing the harassing. One way is to step in directly when someone is being harassed and confront the harasser, pointing out why the behavior is not appropriate. However, this is not always possible, especially if there is a group of individuals involved. Another option is to create a diversion and try to interrupt the harasser and remove them from the incident.

You never know when you will have the opportunity to be an ally for someone else. No matter what the issue, you will grow and learn from it as well as show support for others. What's more, even if you are already a member of one ERG, you can also be an ally for another. When I was part of the steering committee for my LGBTQ+ ERG, I was approached by a woman from another part of the company to help her start a community to champion femininity in the workplace. She believed that there was a double standard in business, and particularly at our company, where aggressive men were praised for being strong and assertive, while a woman who did the same thing was called pushy, annoying, or even occasionally a bitch. She wanted to establish a group to explore how women could express femininity yet also be strong and assertive in order to achieve career advancement at the same rate as men.

I was completely supportive of her plan but asked whether she thought I was the right person to lead this effort, since I had not been promoted within the organization as a woman nor had I fought the battles women face coming up in the organization. I did not want to weaken her efforts if other women criticized the group because its sponsor hadn't "paid her dues." She said I was exactly the person she wanted because I had experienced both the male and now the female sides of workplace behavior. I accepted her explanation and agreed to become her sponsor and act as an ally for her. She called the effort the HER Project and we set about identifying important issues to raise and discuss as a group.

If anyone had ever told me that the first trans executive at my company would be sponsoring the women's femininity project, I would have thought they were crazy! Yet our ERG had great success when we scheduled meetings that featured YouTube videos by Sheryl Sandberg and others, tackling how women are perceived and how they can progress in companies like ours. We started with monthly meetings, the first of which had around 50 attendees with only a few days' notice (the HR department had prevented us from promoting the meeting further in advance because it thought it might overshadow its larger women's ERG, which hadn't had much happening). HR actually required that our new group become a subset of the larger women's ERG, conveniently allowing HR to claim some credit for our work. And while company politics began to constrain our efforts, we persevered. There was such lively discussion and frank sharing from the audience at that first meeting that we had to cut off the debate when we had gone well over our allotted time.

The second event had 150 attendees and we actually ran out of food due to the enthusiasm and higher than expected attendance. We introduced a book club as well. The third meeting had over 300 attendees. I moderated a panel of female vice presidents to discuss their careers and how they had advanced through the ranks, and I answered questions from the audience. For me, this was a wonderful opportunity to help another group within the company and it heightened my awareness of issues and roadblocks to the advancement of women.

The checklist of support at work

Just like you did in Chapter 1, think through who your potential allies can be in your current workplace. Ask yourself the following questions:

- Will my boss be my ally?

- Is there someone in HR who will be my ally?

- Is there an existing diversity and inclusion group within HR?

- Will my friends support my transition and have my back when I'm not around to defend myself?

- Will they help me understand what other people are saying about my transition?

- Is there an existing LGBTQ+ ERG at my company?

- Would my company allow me to start a new ERG?

CHAPTER 9

DEALING WITH DIFFICULT PEOPLE

Dr. Renee McLaughlin has worked at Cigna, the global health insurance company, for a good chunk of her career. She feels her company is generally respectful of diversity, and that there are many visible LGBTQ+ employees in leadership positions. She transitioned at work about four years ago. Interestingly, she told me that her initial thought was to resign from her job before she transitioned, but her HR department talked her into staying. So while she had some reservations, she also had high hopes that they would continue to embrace her after she transitioned.

At the time, Renee thought the transition went, in her words, "exceptionally well." She planned out a strategy with her HR department a full year before she made her initial declaration to the rest of senior management. She had a great ally in place throughout: at the time, the head of diversity and inclusion was an African-American Hispanic lesbian. There was an LGBTQ+ ERG set up, and she was already a member.

After the transition when she first came back, Renee told me that there was a period of time when everyone was getting used to addressing her with her new name and using the right pronouns, but nothing disrespectful happened from either her colleagues or her customers. She continued to climb the corporate ladder, and genuinely likes her job as a senior executive. So she was quite surprised when one day, just before President Trump was elected, and a full three years after her transition, she experienced her first instance of harassment.

Renee was walking down the hall at the corporate headquarters in Chattanooga, TN, and ran into a colleague she hadn't seen in a while but who definitely knew she had transitioned. This man looked at her and paused, and then called her by her male name, which she hadn't used in three years.

Renee was caught off guard, and she was devastated. She told me, "It just floored me. But I wasn't going to tolerate that kind of behavior. Shortly afterwards, I did push that episode through an ethics complaint."

Renee handled the situation appropriately and was able to move on and eventually forget about the incident. Others have not been as lucky. According to Dr. Asa Radix, the experience of transitioning at work is not always positive. Many of his patients, both trans men and trans women, have been forced to endure hateful language and bias. In his words, "I've had people who worked at fairly liberal organizations where, to their face, had really negative comments made, or all of a sudden they weren't getting the promotion they expected. I've had folks who were actually assaulted, and even sexually assaulted at work. I've also had a trans woman recently tell me that in her job, within a healthcare setting, she's made to wear an ID badge with her old name on it because she hasn't legally changed her name. I explained to her that she had every right to use her new name, but what made me so upset was that she didn't think that she had that right."

When I first returned after my initial facial feminization surgery, I didn't notice that I was treated any differently by management than I was before. I was never particularly outspoken, argumentative, or confrontational with people, and I simply went back to work. My second facial surgery took place six months later. When I told my boss that I would be taking a brief medical leave for a week immediately before Christmas, planning to recover during the Christmas to New Year period, his response was to ask if I would then be *"finally* done." He followed up by asking if this would be the "last" medical leave I would need. It was not a comfortable conversation and was not the last awkward interaction I would have with senior management.

My intention in this chapter is not to dissuade you from making a decision that could positively affect every other aspect of your life. From my research, I would say that most of the folks who have transitioned in the workplace have been met with positive responses, and that the negative responses have been subtle. This has been especially true for the people who live in progressive cities within states that provide a full complement of legal protections. But it is better to be prepared for people who will not treat you well after your transition. What's more, their behavior may subtly or overtly affect the way you do, and think about, your job.

The difference between working in a truly supportive environment versus a tolerant one is stark. Some corporations are much more open about celebrating and encouraging diversity and go far beyond their legal requirements. Others pay lip service to their requirements, and at the same time, foster an environment that is neither diverse nor inclusive. In my case, I didn't realize what real diversity and inclusion looked like until I attended conferences about workplace efforts in this regard. For instance, Salesforce has created the new senior position of Chief Equality Officer, currently held by Tony Prophet, who reports directly to the Chief Executive Officer. In this position, he has posted a video called *Proudly Me* (www.youtube.com/watch?v=BKjq-o9FFXs), and its motivational message can empower anyone to bring their full, authentic self to work and succeed. With the enthusiastic backing of the Chairman and CEO, Marc Benioff, Salesforce is considered one of the most inclusive and welcoming companies in the US, and frequently listed as one of the "best places to work" due to its diverse and inclusive corporate culture.

As I've noted before, there are inclusion policies, and then there is the way an organization actually behaves. My own experience left me feeling less than supported. My employer knew its legal responsibilities and recognized the value of my performance, but (at least as I perceived) was overly sensitive to what it perceived as the "distractions" that my transition may have created. I believe that I continued to support my team, my company and its mission with the same dedication and strong results that had characterized my entire eight-year tenure. Unfortunately, notwithstanding the company's addition of a core value of "inclusion" among its published statement of principles, it became clear to me that—at least among senior managers like myself—the leadership did not always conform to their own declared core values.

Aron Janssen, a psychiatrist at NYU Langone Health in New York City, sees variation in acceptance of trans employees that may be tied more to the type of work you do, and less to where you do it. He told me, "The folks that I have who are in STEM [Science, Technology, Engineering and Math] fields have had in general less trouble, particularly in computer science. I would say folks who are more in retail or customer service-oriented positions have reported that there has been more overt hostility and discrimination, even in the New York area." He has also noticed that there is a wariness on the part of employers about possible surgeries and time away from work, just as I experienced, and managing those things has limited the employment options for some of his patients.

The same strategy of "expect the best, be prepared for the worst" holds true in this case. Know your rights and be prepared to use the ammunition that is available to you to respond appropriately and take action when necessary. Dr. Janssen taught me that with any type of relationship there are always complications, and being trans at work and dealing with others is no different from any other type of relationship. Sometimes things go well and sometimes they don't.

As long as you are aware of the potential complications and consider what to do if they arise, you will be better prepared and, it is hoped, have better outcomes.

As you learned in Chapter 3, as a transgender individual you are a member of a protected class and you cannot lose your job just because you have publicly identified as trans. But that doesn't mean that certain individuals will not try to make your life difficult. The issues Renee and I have faced, and dozens of other large and small and unnecessary instances of harassment, bullying, humiliation, and more passive-aggressive behavior, like refusing to use correct name or pronouns, all present a similar challenge: how to deal with the difficult people—or outdated or unprogressive policies with respect to LGBTQ+ rights—in the office. In this chapter, you will learn how to handle a wide variety of workplace dramas, and when to call in the HR department and how its staff can best respond.

YOU ARE NOT A DISTRACTION

You cannot control what an employer or any employee may perceive as a "distraction," and it is not your fault that other people may be distracted at work by your transition. It is the co-workers or managers who may be (or may be perceived to be) "distracted" and will need to make the necessary accommodations in order to get back to work, not the employee in transition. Remember, when you transition in the workplace it is not your responsibility to change others' perceptions. Usually, the HR department assumes responsibility for managing the impact of your transition on the rest of your colleagues with appropriate programming, as we discussed in Chapter 4.

However, this does bring up the larger issue of how far the transitioning employee needs to go to educate others regarding the specifics of being transgender and the logistics

---

of a transition. Many transgender individuals feel that the non-LGBTQ+ community needs to make an effort to educate themselves about LGBTQ+ issues, and that it should not always be our responsibility to ensure their understanding. I believe that a proper balance can be achieved if everyone does their part. The transitioning employee needs to take some responsibility, and the HR department and perhaps the LGBTQ+ ERG or workplace allies can provide the necessary support. Of course, the more trans people can do to educate others, the better off we will be. There will always be questions raised about your change, but we mustn't feel guilty about not being able to completely eliminate any distractions we may cause.

There will be difficult people

If you think that the way you are being treated is affecting your ability to do your job or the performance of your team, that's when you need to call in HR. Overt harassment is the most classic problem, and can include publicly ridiculing or humiliating you, bullying, and other behavior, like refusing to use your preferred name and gender identity or pronoun. One MTF engineer I know who worked for an electric power company in California told me that after her transition some men in her office and contractors began talking down to her as if she was a complete idiot and kept making derogatory comments about women. On the one hand, she was pleased she passed and her gender expression was convincing; but on the other, she wasn't prepared for what women have been facing for years.

When these problems occur, as in Renee's case, your best course of action is to inform HR or your manager about the harassment, especially if it is a clear and overt transgression. If the situation is unclear or of a delicate nature, you could also confide in a trusted ally. We are supposed to rely on the HR department to address the offender and enforce company policies. However, if you work in an environment or state where there are fewer protections, you can still go to HR and report the problem, but if the company still does not protect your emotional and physical safety and well-being, then you may need to seek outside help from an attorney or another support or advocacy organization like the ACLU.

Workplace discrimination is a separate issue from harassment. Most workplaces understand their legal requirements and would be foolish to overtly discriminate, such as firing you after your transition, or not accepting a job application. However, as with the friend I mentioned in Chapter 7, who worked at the Fortune 500 company and was not considered for a promotion, these things do happen. A more common occurrence may be a change to your suggested pattern of involvement in key activities at work, such that you get fewer opportunities to be part of decision-making or less face-to-face time with clients and customers. In these instances, consult your attorney or the Transgender Law Center and know your rights before you address HR or your manager. If your concerns are not resolved and even if you're not working in a state with progressive protections, the EEOC can still help you fight against discrimination by making a formal claim. Refer to Chapter 3 for more details about legal remedies if you feel you are being discriminated against.

Regardless of whether you feel harassed or discriminated against, and even if the HR department is not protecting you and satisfactorily addressing the situation, be resolute and don't apologize or back down from presenting with your chosen gender expression. There is a solution for every problem, but you need to get outside legal assistance, understand your options, and consider the long- and short-term implications of various courses of action.

The bathroom drama

Another unfortunate issue remains in today's workplace: what to do about the restroom. This can be the source of anxiety and significant drama. The popular and ground-breaking Amazon Prime series, *Transparent*, which tells the story of a transgender woman and her family, depicted the nightmare scenario of a trans woman who is confronted in a women's bathroom for being "obviously a male" and is threatened with calling security if she doesn't leave. Although this scenario appeared in a work of fiction, the fear of a similar encounter does run through the mind of many trans people, especially early in their transition when they are out in public.

The most progressive companies encourage and expect transitioning employees to use the bathroom of their choice and may have gender-neutral bathrooms. Barneys New York store in San Francisco has made all its restrooms gender neutral, and an article posted in 2017 in *Mic* entitled *There are more than 160,000 US businesses with gender-neutral restrooms* drives the point home.[1]

If your company does not have a clear policy regarding restrooms for transgender employees, it will need to make one. Clarify your preference when you declare your transition. You can tell your boss and HR department that you intend to use the bathroom of your preferred identity. If they do not accept your decision, then ask them to make arrangements for you to use a private bathroom, and if the answer is still "no," then they are sending a clearly discriminatory signal.

While this is a major consideration for the transgender community, there may be times when mistakes are made, and you might be at fault. Early after my transition, I caught myself as I was walking into the men's restroom by mistake—force of habit after eight years of working in the same building. And I once heard a story about a transgender woman who was arguing with a male colleague in a meeting. They continued to have their heated exchange during a break, and she followed him right into the men's room, because that's what she had been used to doing.

---

1   https://mic.com/articles/180693/there-are-more-than-160000-us-businesses-
    with-gender-neutral-restrooms#.bp8acS8hb.

Understanding changes in your performance evaluation

At work, it shouldn't matter who you are or how you appear. Even if you look drastically different following your transition, the company should expect the same performance. However, this is not always the case. Many co-workers don't know what to make of trans people, and their conscious or unconscious bias may come between you and doing your job. What's more, you may not just be compared to other men or women in your office, you may be compared to the perception of your old self before the transition. This may be more important if you were previously a high performer and are being reviewed as the new you. Often, employers do not consider everything that a transitioning employee has been going through: medical issues, family struggles, divorce, moving to a new home, and so on. Therefore, whether or not they can or want to take these outside influences into account, you need to be focused on what you can control at work. So you must stay sharp in all your required competencies so as not to give anyone a reason to say your performance has suffered after your transition.

Tiffany, the training and professional development coordinator, knows of many trans individuals with other employers or companies who have been fired or "downsized" out of a job in a move that was directly related to their trans status, despite the fact that it is illegal. These companies assume that most people just will not have the money or stamina to battle their employer's illegal business practices in court. A much more common scenario occurs when a company wants to eliminate an individual employee—transgender or otherwise—and just gradually "performance manages" them out. This practice can be directly tied to a yearly performance review.

There are usually two sides of performance evaluations: the self-assessment, which includes how you feel about yourself and your work; and the manager assessment, or how your work is judged by management. Both of these assessments are critical for ensuring that your career will continue to progress after you've transitioned. When you are crafting your goals for the year, focus on clear and quantitative objectives that you will meet. Then in your self-assessment, you can clearly point to your measurable accomplishments. Include specifics of timeframes for completing tasks and avoid the use of subjective assessments which may be interpreted in ways that could be biased against you.

Objective goals are clear: if you were supposed make ten widgets an hour, and you did so every day, and are able to track your production, then no one can argue with your performance. However, if your goals are more subjective and hard to measure, such as "engages and works well with customers" or "is an effective team leader," it leaves room for nebulous interpretation. Even in those cases, if you can match the subjective goal with an objective one, such as making a certain number of sales calls or achieving a certain dollar target of sales, you will be better off.

When I returned to the office after my first surgery, I was intent on performing my job exactly the way I used to, just with my new body. I was, however, less than completely confident about the way I was presenting and, in retrospect, that uncertainty may have caused me to become more reserved in the office. I was particularly worried about the reaction to my somewhat different voice and how my appearance was perceived in meetings. I worried about whether my transition was going to be a distraction to the team. Relatively soon it sank in that I had a great group of co-workers and subordinates and that I didn't need to worry about my voice or my appearance. What others thought of the way I looked didn't determine how I engaged with my work. Whether or not I was meeting my goals for femininity was my personal issue, but in the office the things that mattered were how I did my job and that I was comfortable with myself.

Unfortunately, I learned during my first mid-year review after the transition that the benchmarks for my performance review had changed. My department continued to perform just as well as ever. We met all of our goals and my team reported that I was supporting them. I crafted my self-assessment to reflect all of the positive accomplishments my team and I had achieved. The feedback I received, however, was not in sync with those accomplishments. I was told that I was "not as engaged" as I had been. My manager told me that although the organization could not "put [its] finger on the problem," something was "missing" in my performance. When I asked which of my objective goals had not been met, neither my manager nor HR could point to any. When I asked for an example that would demonstrate my perceived lack of engagement or that some aspect my performance was "missing," they could not provide one. The fact was that my results were excellent and my team was happy.

While the company's issue seems obvious in hindsight, at the time I was at a loss. I was determined to improve my communications and make an effort to appear more engaged at work, because the negative review shook my confidence. I began to wonder if I really had substantive issues in my work. I had trouble believing that the demanding company in which I had thrived for eight years might have changed its view of me and was trying to "manage me out."

I do recognize that during the initial few months after I returned from that first surgery, I was somewhat tentative and unsure of how my co-workers would perceive me. Those anxieties possibly led me to exhibit less of an "executive presence" than others had previously perceived. Presenting as a woman was new to me, and the issues I was having in my non-work life—divorce, my kids, the medical aspects of my transition—likely impacted my interactions with co-workers. I now believe that a trained, professional member of the HR staff should have anticipated such issues and assisted me, as an employee in transition, in coping with these sorts of issues. Unfortunately, the fact of my transition was new to the HR department as well, and its ability to deal with it was less than optimal.

My year-end performance review came six months later. Again, all objective goals were met and I was perceived as somewhat "improving" in my "engagement." I continued in my efforts to project confidence and engagement. I remained energetic and available for my teams. During the next mid-year review, once again, I had met all my goals, but management began talking about "succession planning" for my team. I was asked to put some ideas together to develop my most promising senior leaders. The company was planning for my departure, though I did not immediately catch on to that fact. I continued to believe, perhaps naively, that the company had my best interests and long-term career goals in mind.

At the next year-end review, I was told I had done a great job and nearly exceeded expectations. I took the review as an excellent sign that all was again right with my relationship with the company. I attributed my success to my conscious effort to appear more engaged, and to regularly communicate my accomplishments to senior management. I believed that senior management was becoming comfortable with me as a woman. At this point, it had been 19 months since my first declaration about my transition. I thought I had made my way back into everyone's good graces.

Within two months I was passed over for a promotion for which, I believed, I was better qualified. Without any notice, it went to a former peer (and, I had thought, a friend) who would now be my new boss. During my first meeting with that new boss, I heard again about my supposed "lack of engagement" problem! Reality finally hit. I was never going to enjoy the same career support and opportunities I had before. It was time for me to go.

Had I wanted to stay, there is not much I could have done differently. My ammunition was basically what I had accomplished— the objective results of my group's overall success. All of the criticisms had nothing to do with my objective performance or that of my team. I was done fighting for my job there. I started returning calls from recruiters, who frequently contacted me about opportunities in my line of work. Within a few months, I was offered a great new position at another smaller company in the biotech industry.

I've already had my first performance assessment at my new company, Rigel. In my self-assessment, I had written what I had accomplished in the first six months. This time, the management review was completely different.

Here are the highlights: "I think of Dana's hire as a game-changing event for Rigel...Dana's technical expertise, her formidable experience in dealing with health authorities, great management skills, desire to influence discussions beyond the regulatory aspect of a decision, her sense of initiative, level-headed approach, excellent ability to explain challenging situations and interact with everyone, including peers, colleagues of the executive team, and more junior collaborators, have made her a trusted and influential senior executive. In addition, she inspires the department by her strong work ethic. She has always met and often exceeded the goals and expectations. It's a pleasure working with you. And I look forward to our collaboration in bringing continuous success to Rigel in the next year."

Take action: ask for a 360 review

If you disagree with your performance review, first ask for concrete, objective examples of the performance issues raised. You are well within your rights to ask, "Can you give me an example of what exactly you were looking for, or what I didn't do that I should have?"

Your next recourse may be to ask for a 360 review. This is an HR practice that takes into account more than just your opinion and that of your managers. A 360 review is when HR interviews your superiors, colleagues, and subordinates and collects information on your strengths and weaknesses to provide a more subjective insight to your performance. It is not unreasonable to ask for this, and they can be done more or less formally. I've had it done a few times over my career, and I've done it for several of my employees to help their career development.

However, be prepared to live with the consequences. If you initiate a 360 review to get more feedback from people besides your boss about how the rest of the organization feels you're performing, they better have your back, or at least be able to quantify your performance.

MAYBE IT IS YOU?

Think very carefully whether your difficulties at work are caused by something other than discrimination or harassment before you take legal action. This is where support from a trusted confidante, ally, or outside legal advice can be helpful. It is in the realm of possibility that your transition really is taking your attention away from your job to such an extent that you can no longer manage both. The best way to determine if there is a real problem is to compare your behavior and actions to your job description. Be completely objective. If you're late for work nine times out of ten, or you're missing deadlines or handing in work that is below par, those may be measurable objective criteria that represent real evidence of your inability to perform.

You don't have to stand for poor behavior

Many people who transition end up leaving their employer. Some say they wanted a clean break or to start their life anew, and that's a viable option if you are dealing with difficult people or a workplace that does not value you. Luckily, you'll see in the next chapter that there are plenty of businesses, including the federal government as well as large and small corporations, that actively recruit trans people.

There are plenty of people who have great transitions and don't deal with any negativity. But if you do, be prepared. If you are facing overt or insidious discrimination, you have legal recourse.

CHAPTER 10

MAKING YOUR NEXT MOVE

In the best-case scenario, your transition is a big success. The company embraces the new you, and so do your colleagues and customers. But what do you do if you are not as lucky? Or, what do you do if you now realize that you are not in the right company or situation to transition? If you've carefully considered the information in this book, you may see your workplace in a different light. If the people at your current job will never graciously accept your preferred gender expression or if your company does not cover the health benefits you need, you might want to look for a new position before you even transition. In either case, there are best practices to search for a better workplace environment where you can be your most authentic self.

In some scenarios, managing your career by starting with a clean slate just before or right after a transition can be a powerful and empowering action to take.

The stay or go checklist

It doesn't matter why you want to look for a new job. Many transitioning employees want to make a fresh start at a new company, or in a new division of their old company, or have been forced directly or indirectly by their employers to make this decision, as you learned in the last chapter. You should never feel guilty about searching for a new job. Whether or not you are trans, it is important to make the best choices for your career development and for your personal satisfaction.

I've also repeatedly seen through my research for this book that once someone decides to transition, their perspective on their current job or company can change. You may become more self-aware, or begin to look at your company in a different—positive or negative—light. As you examine all the pieces that need to come together in order for you to express your preferred gender identity and be your authentic self, you may for the first time see the shortcomings of your organization.

Before you announce your intention to leave, review the questions below. There may be one overriding reason to stay where you are that will change your perspective, at least for the time being. You can also use these questions to determine how and why another employer might be the right place for you to thrive after you transition, or would be a better place to start one.

By evaluating a company from a more trans-knowledgeable perspective, you will be able to assess if it will be a better overall fit. For example, I accepted the fact that I would have to pay for my surgical procedures as the company I worked for explicitly excluded coverage for transgender procedures at that time. It never occurred to me to see if other companies in the biotech industry were covering these expenses, because I still enjoyed my job and the mission of the company, and I wasn't aware of other trans people in the industry who could have broadened my perspective. However, if health insurance coverage is essential for your transition, you can focus on companies that have support mechanisms for LGBTQ+ employees already in place, like an LGBTQ+ ERG, and you can enquire if these allies know if the company also offers health insurance that will cover the cost of a medical transition. For me, when I started my latest job search, I wanted a company where the culture was more accepting of all types of diversity, so it was meaningful to me that the CEO of my new company was openly gay. While his status may not matter as much to everyone, as a trans person, once I knew this small detail I immediately felt more comfortable.

These are some of the special considerations you should take into consideration as you begin your search for a new position:

- Are you living in a progressive or high-equality state (see Chapter 3) where you have career opportunities and important legal protections against discrimination in hiring, as well as access to accommodations?

- Are you in an industry that is traditionally more progressive with respect to diversity and inclusion (see Chapter 4)?

- Are your skills transferrable to a different industry that may be more progressive?

- Are you living in a high-equality state that mandates health insurance or prevents exclusion of health insurance coverages specifically for transgender care?

- Does your current company offer the health insurance you need?

- Are you currently undergoing a treatment regimen such as hormone therapy or electrolysis that needs to be maintained?

- Does your current company have an LGBTQ+ ERG?

- Does your current company provide anti-discrimination and anti-harassment training for all managers and employees?

- Does your HR department have clear diversity and inclusion policies?

- Does your company have a diversity and inclusion group?

- Do you have the appropriate savings or financial support to cover your expenses while you look for a new job?

- Do you have bonuses or other forms of compensation that are payable in the future?

- Do you have unused vacation time?

My story

I stayed in my job for two years after my transition for a few reasons. First, I liked the work that I was doing, and I believed in the company's overall mission to provide life-saving therapies to patients with unmet medical needs. I really cared about my team, I had great allies across the company, and there was a lot of positivity around me. There was a time, ten months or so after my transition, when I began to feel really good about myself. I remember clearly the moment when I decided that I was feeling proud of who I had become and I wasn't going to worry any longer about my voice or appearance. I'm just going to be Dana. That sustained me for a while, but the way management was treating me continued to bother me and finally pushed me to consider other options.

I felt my career had stalled, and I thought maybe I just should accept that reality and stick it out, but then I went to the Out & Equal Executive Forum in March 2017. This non-profit organization is dedicated to achieving LGBTQ+ workplace equality, and this was one of its important senior level conferences which are held annually. I'd heard about the conference from other people in our LGBTQ+ ERG. My company was an official sponsor of the event, but management wasn't planning on sending a representative from the company. To me, that decision was just another way it showed that diversity and LGBTQ+ rights were not a priority for the company.

As annoyed as I was about that, I still wanted to go and so I offered to be the company representative. I thought it could even show my company in a more positive light since I would represent it. I didn't ask for any special consideration from my boss and was able to clear my calendar for most of the conference, which took place in San Francisco about 15 miles from work. We were already entitled to a free registration because we were sponsors. And yet, true to form, when I put in a reimbursement for the day's parking, my boss initially didn't sign off on it, because he didn't think attending the conference was particularly important for my job. When I explained the purpose of the meeting he begrudgingly signed off on the reimbursement form.

At the beginning of the conference, I attended a breakout meeting of sponsor executives. We were asked to each take a turn and tell the group how we handled a moment of courage that occurred in our lives, either inside or outside work. There were about 40 executives, and my turn came around the halfway point. Some people shared a courageous moment at work and others told personal stories. There were some very impressive people in the room, including a lesbian woman who was divorced and became the first to petition the California courts for joint child custody, well before marriage equality legislation was passed.

When it was my turn to talk, I told my "nail polish and earrings" story that triggered my official declaration to transition. When I told that story, everyone's jaws dropped. They couldn't believe that an HR department at a "progressive company" would treat an employee in such a cold manner. Denise Visconti, the employment attorney I interviewed for this book who advises companies about harassment and discrimination, was in that room. When it was her turn to speak, she said she was an attorney who advised "companies not to do what Dana's company did to her."

Afterwards, the woman who was running that executive group told my story to the head of the whole conference, and then asked if I would retell my story to everyone attending. This time, there were 200 people in the room. Again, the whole room was silent and somewhat visibly dumbfounded that an HR department would do that at a Fortune 100 company. Once I saw that there was clear and enormous LGBTQ+ support and progressive thinking at other companies, I realized that I didn't have to accept my apparent career stall. Instead, I came to see that I still had value another company might appreciate, because I knew that I was very good at my job and I had a lot to offer. But most importantly, I realized that I didn't have to put up with poor treatment. Ever. The more I learned about other companies in and out of my industry, and talked to people who had transitioned and saw that their experience at work was different from mine, the more excited I became about the prospect of starting a new job search. By the end of the two-day conference I caught myself thinking more than once, "It's time to move on."

After the conference, I started answering recruiters' calls. I had always been on their radar, believing that it was important to maintain relationships with them, but I had gone dark right after I transitioned, because I wasn't out as Dana on social media, including LinkedIn. But after the conference the first thing I did was change my LinkedIn profile to reflect what I wanted to be: a transgender advocate. After that, I was completely out, and it was clear that at least I was a woman looking for a new job.

Soon after, I got a call from a recruiter, who pitched me a new position and also asked if I would talk with him about an LGBTQ+ non-profit organization he was involved with. I agreed to speak with him, and from there we began talking more seriously. I pondered whether I needed to disclose my transgender status to him, but eventually decided that I was already out in social media, so I might as well. I then asked him if he knew I was transgender, and he told me he had seen my LinkedIn profile. He told me he didn't consider my being trans an obstacle, was impressed with my career accomplishments, and said other companies would welcome a competent employee like me. Although I also knew it shouldn't matter to an employer that I was trans, it was good to hear it from him and that further encouraged and empowered me to pursue other options.

Eventually, he told me about a position at Rigel, a much smaller research and discovery-focused biotech company that was looking to build a development capability. Even though it had been in business for more than 20 years, it wanted to develop and market its own drugs for rare diseases, and wanted me to help gain FDA approval. It had begun to put together a team of executives who could help the company move in this direction.

The recruiter convinced me to talk to the Chief Medical Officer to learn more about the company's needs and what the corporate culture was like. I really enjoyed speaking with her, and was even more interested when I learned that the CEO, Raul Rodriguez, was out as a gay man. The fact that it was a small company was a plus for me. I was excited about the challenge of building a team from the ground up the way I wanted. The company also supported the idea of my LGBTQ+ advocacy work. In fact, the CEO participated in the AIDS/LifeCycle, which is a big fundraising event in the Bay Area for the San Francisco AIDS Foundation where cyclists ride more than 500 miles from San Francisco to Los Angeles once a year. This reassured me that Rigel was committed to LGBTQ+ diversity and inclusion. After a bit of negotiation, I accepted the position.

Working at my current position is a night-and-day difference from my previous situation. At Rigel, the staff completely accept me, value my knowledge and years of experience and see my potential to help them build their future. It is so refreshing when senior management actually respects your position, wants to know what you think, and appreciates your contributions regardless of your gender expression. In addition, I made three key new hires, one of whom knew me before my transition, and one who knew me both before and after. All three have welcomed the opportunity to work for me based upon my leadership style and our positive camaraderie as a team, irrespective of my gender identity.

CHANGE YOUR PAPERWORK BEFORE YOU APPLY FOR A NEW JOB

There were some other steps I took to lay the groundwork for my job search because I had already transitioned. First, I needed to make sure that all of my credentials reflected my new name and gender. All of my HR documentation had long been changed, but I now had to consider contacting previous employers in case a new employer wanted to check my references. I started by updating my college degrees and my medical credentials. Then I got in touch with some of my previous employers and anyone I would ask for a personal reference.

I also updated my resume and all of my social media accounts, like LinkedIn. Not only did I change my name, but I added information about my outside activities and advocacy work that indicated my trans status. I used words that would signal that I was transgender. If you look at my LinkedIn, I don't profile myself as, "Proud transgender woman." Instead, it reads, "Pharmaceutical executive, transgender advocate."

Your resume is a snapshot of your professional history, and it's what you want people to know about you. Since I've been hiring for my own team at Rigel, I've seen more and more resumes that include community service commitments, and I've found it offers a great opportunity to discover other aspects of a candidate's life and what is important to them. I highly recommend adding this to your resume and social media accounts.

Preparing for recruiters and potential new employers

Large and midsize corporations use professional recruiters as their gatekeepers for job applicants. You do not have to tell a recruiter or a potential employer during an interview that you have transitioned or intend to transition. And, a potential new employer cannot ask you about your gender expression or sexual orientation. However, I wanted to be completely transparent, so I made sure that the recruiter knew I was trans.

According to Ken Eng, a professional recruiter in the technology and biotech industries, companies are more cognizant of making sure that they hire underrepresented minorities, including LGBTQ+ employees. However, a recruiter's job is to bring in the best candidates for the position each company is looking to fill: they are not going to push your application forward if you are not a good fit for a position just because you are in an underrepresented minority.

Ken works in the Bay Area and recruits exclusively for a prestigious tech company known to be one of the most progressive companies and a leader in valuing diversity and inclusion. He has worked with several transgender individuals, and reports that he treats everyone equally. As an Asian-American, he told me that when he is recruiting, he realizes that he has a bias toward promoting underrepresented minorities, and would like to see more underrepresented minorities in the workforce.

Ken suggests that one of the best ways for any potential employee to see if they are a fit for a different employer is to get a good sense of the culture. The company's website is a great place to start, and you can also talk directly to the recruiter about your concerns without revealing that you are trans, if that is your choice. For instance, if you don't want to be out to your recruiter, you can ask them about the overall company culture. Ken told me, "I always tell applicants that before the interview they need to do their homework. See if the new company sponsors employee resource groups. Look beyond the website: is this company participating in LGBT events? Are there articles about it on other sites? Then, check out Glassdoor.com, a website where employees and former employees anonymously review companies and their management. You can also connect with existing employees via LinkedIn or Facebook to see how they like their job and the corporate culture. Ask what is their favorite part of their job, and what are some things they would want to change.

"You can also talk frankly with your recruiter or interviewer about corporate culture. Cultural fit is such a huge part of someone's longevity and their happiness and their productivity at a company. It's feeling like they're at home. You can ask if the company engages in community service, or if there are employee resource groups that the company forms for all the various types of employees that they have. Be very direct about asking if there are activities that the company does as a whole to support."

The best recruiters build relationships for the long term, and that's something to look for when you are evaluating your relationship with one. You can tell if you are working with a good recruiter if they are really invested in talking with you and not just going through the motions. Are they asking you a lot of questions about you and your experience? Are they taking the time to get to know you? Are they digging deeper, rather than just scratching the surface, when they're getting to know your professional history? Ken told me, "A good recruiter really connects with the candidates. Regardless of whether or not I can take that person right now, every candidate has a story. Every person has something to share, and I think the best recruiters not only look at that story for the short term, but can see long-term potential. Maybe we don't have a position right now for the person, but if you can see that person belongs at a particular company, you will do everything you can to set it up where they eventually find a position. I want my candidates to stay in touch with me no matter where they land."

Ken also believes that it's very important to be able to represent yourself in the truest sense, and not to worry that there will be a backlash if you add something to your resume that may lead someone to believe that you're transgender. In fact, knowing this upfront can save time wasted in the wrong job or working for the wrong company.

Lastly, Ken encourages transgender individuals trying to get into the workforce for the first time, or even those who are more seasoned, to bring their authentic self to work. He told me, "I tell my clients to show up the way they really want to show up, and that passion will come through during an interview. I mean owning your truth and living that, and not stopping until you find that environment that is going to be where you are able to thrive and succeed. Do not settle for a company that really doesn't have your best interests at heart, both professionally and personally."

COME TO ANY INTERVIEW PREPARED

Regardless whether you've transitioned or not, come prepared to any interview. An interview is the beginning of a relationship, and just like when you meet new people, you show a lot more interest when you're the one asking questions. If the healthcare benefit package is really important to you, ask about it. The best recruiters really like candidates who ask a lot of questions and it helps them discover what is truly motivating that person to want to apply for a particular position.

The best companies to work for

The best companies to work for may have many young employees, and gender expression or LGBTQ+ status doesn't matter as much to them. Some even go out of their way to recruit top LGBTQ+ talent. However, there are some companies who talk the talk, without walking the walk. Just because a company promotes on their website that it embraces diversity and inclusion, doesn't mean it does. It may want to in the future, but those policies may not be in place at the present.

It may be difficult to determine whether a company that promotes itself as having a high degree of diversity and inclusion actually follows through. The best way to find out, again, is to do your homework. Ask your recruiter or interviewer about the company's diversity policies.

The following companies currently promote their diversity and inclusion policies and practices, at the time of writing this book. It is not meant to be an inclusive list, and some companies that promote themselves as diverse and inclusive may be more aspirational than referring to what actually occurs in their culture. Always look deeper and try to verify as many specifics as you can about these types of statements by checking directly with your current or potential future employer about its existing trans-friendly policies.

- Aetna
- Air Products
- AlixPartners
- Allstate
- Altria
- American Airlines
- AmerisourceBergen
- Apple
- Aramark
- Arconic
- AstraZeneca
- AT&T
- Bank of America

- Bayer
- Best Buy
- BlackRock
- BNY Mellon
- Boeing
- Capital One
- CBRE
- Chemours
- Chervon
- Chubb
- Cisco
- Citibank
- Clorox

- CNA

- Comcast

- Cracker Barrel

- Darden

- Dell

- Deloitte

- Direct Energy

- Dow Chemical

- DuPont

- Ernst & Young (EY)

- ExxonMobil

- First Data

- Freddie Mac

- Genentech

- General Electric (GE)

- General Motors

- Google

- Grant Thornton

- GSK

- Hewlett-Packard (HP)

- Hilton

- HSBC

- Huntington Ingalls Industries

- IBM

- Intel

- Intuit

- Johnson & Johnson

- JPMorgan Chase

- Leidos

- Littler Mendelson P.C.

- Lockheed Martin

- Marriott

- Marsh & McLennan

- MassMutual

- McDonald's

- Merck

- MGM Resorts

- MillerCoors

- Mondelez

- NGLCC (National LGBT Chamber of Commerce)

- Nissan

- Northrop Grumman

- Oracle

- Paul Hastings
- Pfizer
- Phillips 66
- Praxair
- Protiviti
- Publicis Health
- QBE
- Queerty
- Reed Smith
- Rigel
- Robert Half
- Rockwell Collins
- RSM
- S&P Global
- Salesforce
- Sanofi
- SAP
- SC Johnson
- Sodexo
- Southwest Airlines
- State Street
- State Farm
- T-Mobile
- T. Rowe Price
- Takeda
- Target
- TE Connectivity
- Texas Instruments
- Toyota
- Travelers
- United Technologies
- UPS
- US Federal Government (TSA, USDA, CIA, etc.)
- USAA
- Verizon
- Visa
- Volkswagen Group of America
- Walmart
- Walt Disney Company
- Wawa
- Wells Fargo
- Whirlpool
- Workday

Spotlight on Intel

Intel currently has 107,000 employees that work in many states (Colorado, Oregon, New Mexico, California, Texas, Arizona, and Washington) as well as 46 countries across the globe. Intel currently has a standardized transition process, which allows for effective communications and few disruptions to the workplace.

Intel's goal is to make a transition a partnership between the employee and the company so that it can meet the needs of the employees, and balance its business needs. The process it has developed has been successful due to this partnership approach. Intel's transition protocol includes a PowerPoint presentation and a training set for managers and HR. The PowerPoint is available on its internal internet site, and serves as a briefing package for transgender employees. The company also keeps case studies on file to use as examples of how to handle topics that come up frequently, such as privacy and confidentiality, dress code, restroom use, and understanding personal religious beliefs. It has also created specially trained call center agents who are familiar with all of the protocols and will help guide a transitioning employee through the corporate process. Once a relationship is created through the call center, it stays in place through the employee's entire transition. Intel also offers an optional self-identification survey that is meant to enable HR to better understand the overall LGBTQ+ representation across the US employee population and to provide resources.

Currently, Intel offers gender confirmation surgery as part of its health benefit plan, as well as available financing toward gender-confirming cosmetic interventions. Its policy is consistent with the WPATH standards, but the availability to individual employees is based on which health coverage they sign up for.

Intel offers a "breaking bias" workshop to all employees and managers through its Neuro Leadership Institute. It also trains all of its managers worldwide through an inclusion and leadership program, which provides tools and guidance to different business units and organizations, including diversity playbooks and customized plans. It also supports iGlobe, which is the ERG for LGBTQ+ employees. Additionally, Intel formed a leadership council, Intel Out & Ally Leadership Council, made up of Intel's most senior leaders who advocate for full inclusion of the LGBTQ community. The leadership council and all employee ERG partners promote full inclusion for the LGBTQ community. Intel offers tangible collaterals to allow employees to demonstrate they are an ally. This is done by employees who choose to show support by adding an Ally Badge and pronoun stickers to their employee ID badge.

Spotlight on Facebook

Facebook currently has close to 25,000 employees in the US and is based in Menlo Park, California. Many LGBT+ employees are out at high levels of management. As a company, it has encouraged all LGBTQ employees to self-identify. According to the results of a voluntary annual survey of Facebook's US workforce, which has a 62 percent response rate, 7 percent of people self-identified as either lesbian, gay, bisexual, queer, transgender, or asexual. It offers a global LGBT+ Facebook Resource Group (FBRG) that has individual groups in different locations and roughly 3000 members. There is even a more informal transgender group that acts as a subset of the LGBT+ERG, as well as a "secret" group for people who are not comfortable being out to anyone except other trans employees.

Because the company is based in California, it has a formalized anti-discrimination policy, and offers healthcare that covers employee transitions. Facebook considers its healthcare package to feature industry-leading benefits for transgender employees. A gender transition is considered in the same category as any medical condition, which means there's no dollar maximum. The company's healthcare coverage surpasses the WPATH standards to include non-genital, non-breast surgical interventions, including liposuction, lipo filling, pectoral implants, and other aesthetic procedures. It also covers voice and communication therapy. Regardless of sexual orientation or gender identity, employees have access to a robust fertility benefit that includes adoption assistance, egg freezing, sperm retrieval, in vitro fertilization (IVF), and any IVF costs that are not covered by insurance.

Facebook is also known to take individual needs into account to improve the workplace for all. A good example of this policy was when it moved into its current corporate headquarters, showers were added to all of the buildings, which came about after a request from employees who would exercise before work or at lunch and wanted places to shower on campus. As one of the HR representatives told me, "One of our transgender employees came to us and said, those showers are male and female, and I don't feel comfortable using either one. We were able to convert a handful of those showers into non-gender showers, so either men or women or however you identify, can use that shower. Of course, they have locks, but it's just a very subtle nod to the fact that not everyone identifies as binary."

According to Facebook, the company has clearly defined policies for transitioning and then support for transgender employees beyond the transition. Because of this, there is a strong sense of community both inside and outside the company, not just tolerating someone who identifies as transgender or non-binary, but actually celebrating those differences.

Lastly, Facebook is a supportive participant in Pride festivals and Pride parades around the country and worldwide. Last year, it had over 1500 employees march in the parades globally. Mark Zuckerberg was one of the first Silicon Valley CEOs to march in a Pride parade in 2013, when he rode on the Facebook Pride float.

The LGBTQ+ community in general is referenced in Facebook's unconscious bias training and it also offers ally training. In terms of recruiting, Facebook employs what they call the "Diverse Slate Approach," which encourages hiring managers to consider candidates from underrepresented backgrounds when interviewing for an open position.

Antonia Belcher started her own business

The idea of owning a business is enticing. Many trans people I've met have gone down this route and created a whole new career based on their skills and knowledge. If you are thinking that the existing business options where you live are limited for trans employees, it might be time to consider hanging out your own shingle. Being an entrepreneur is a viable and exciting option if you have the capital and can manage the financial risks involved.

For instance, Antonia Belcher, who we met earlier, transitioned in the early 2000s. She has been in the construction business for her entire career, and worked as a trained and qualified surveyor, project manager, construction engineer, and construction arbitrator.

Antonia transitioned at the only company she had ever worked for. When she decided that it was time to transition, she gave her colleagues a year's notice. At the time, they were looking for new office space, and she gave each of the other six partners in the firm an option: she could stay, or she could leave. Then, she let the other partners come to a group decision. Two months later, one of the partners came to see her and let her know that they wanted her to stay. For the next five years, she helped them build a highly profitable business.

Then, 11 years ago, she decided to start her own company in the same business. She wanted to create her own practice as a trans woman to show the world that trans women can set up and run their own businesses. It took a great leap of faith. Once again, she told her partners, and this time, their response was equally supportive. One of them asked if he could join her new venture. Another junior partner quickly joined. By the time she was ready to leave, she had brought along 18 people—half of the old firm.

Today she reports that business is wonderful. Antonia told me, "I wish I actually had left the other firm beforehand because by doing what I did, it remotivated me because I was that woman running her own show that I wanted to be. My transition also motivated all the people who came across with me. I hadn't seen them so fired up about work in a long time."

The right job fit is out there

No matter what you decide is the best move for you and your career, be assured that the current employment environment is evolving and becoming more friendly and welcoming to members of the LGBTQ+ community, and transgender employees in particular. This happens at different rates in different locations, but the fact remains that it is moving inexorably forward.

As you learned in this chapter, there are many important points to consider as you contemplate a career move, and taking a thorough and systematic approach to assessing your current employment and your personal situation can help you make the best decision. Knowing what to look for in a new employer, how to make your resume attractive, and how to talk to recruiters and new employers can help you assemble the facts you need.

While finding that perfect job may not happen overnight, it does exist; you just have to know how to find it. More importantly, remember that diversity increases a company's profitability, and trans people make great employees.

CHAPTER 11

IT ALL COMES TOGETHER

The other day I was on my computer and found some old pictures of my kids. My wife Stella and I were scrolling through the photos, which were about 15 years old, back when I was David. I was in many of them, and, to be honest, I looked happy. Stella was sweet, and told me, "You were pretty good-looking back then." I said, "Thank you, but seeing them now feels sort of strange."

It was uncomfortable to look at pictures that didn't have the new me in them but I'm taking that as a good sign. When I look in the mirror, I know I made the right decision for me, and that I could never go back to being David. And despite the fact that I have wonderful memories from those days, that life is now over, because that person is just not me. And for that, I'm thankful.

As you now know, my current tranquility and self-acceptance did not exist for some time when I first transitioned. In fact, the arc of a transition takes longer than anyone would expect, and includes both the physical, mental, and emotional facets. While the change in one's gender expression will appear suddenly in the office—for me, it must have seemed as if one day I was a male and the next day I appeared as a female—the internal psychological transition takes more time. Your office will never see the internal turmoil of "before," and the challenge for you will be to maintain an air of calm and grace during the "after."

Like many things in life, this can be easier said than done. It took nearly two years from the time that I first appeared as Dana for me to feel fully comfortable with my new self, and to complete my progression through the behavioral, medical, and surgical changes for my desired transition. Only then was I able to shed my anxiety and insecurity about how I appeared and interacted as a woman.

When you transition, you should be able eventually to eliminate your gender dysphoria. For me, the oestrogen patches and testosterone blockers brought a sense of relief and were the beginning of a long medical journey with important milestones. The very first facial feminization surgery was another big step forward, and then breast implants and finally genital surgery completed my physical changes. With practice of movements and voice training I was beginning to look and sound more like the woman I wanted to be, and it seemed as if every day I was getting closer to the point where I felt settled and content about my persona. Some days it was harder to focus at work; on other days, work was a much-needed distraction from the drama that was happening elsewhere. In every part of my life, I had to adapt to a new normal. It was easy to become distracted by the transition and overwhelmed by the decisions I had to make about how I was showing up at work—both mentally and physically.

I found the best way to deal with all of these changes was to learn to compartmentalize the different aspects of my life, so that when I was at work I could put aside my inner psychological transition and just do my job. I had to divide my life into four sections. I had my work, my family, my transition, and my social life and advocacy work. It felt as if all four parts of my life were changing drastically at the same time, but at different rates, and with different crises to manage. I tried to make sure that the drama from one area didn't affect the others. In truth, it was very, very challenging.

For anyone who is transitioning, there will be a whirlwind of changes and adjustments during those first few years. But by putting blinders on at work during the day, I was able to focus my attention and be productive in the workplace. Any good employee should do the same, regardless of whether they're transitioning: the other turmoil that may be going on in your life, or simply potential distractions you may face, should not impact your best work. Again, that is easier said than done.

For me, the personal side of my life was particularly tumultuous—I was busy trying to maintain a home in California for my children during my transition, as well as helping them cope with the changes that were happening in both their parents' lives. After we divorced, my ex-wife decided to move back to the East Coast, which meant selling the family home and making the children somewhat bi-coastal. There will always be challenging aspects to any divorce and throwing in a transgender parent was more than just another hurdle. Luckily, my relationship with Stella, my current wife, and her children, couldn't have been better. Stella was amazingly supportive during all of my medical and legal challenges, and helped me create a very welcoming environment for my children as well as hers in our new home. Blending families poses its own challenges, but all our kids got along so well it was an unexpected relief, and one less thing I had to worry about. Stella's children are much younger than mine, so it was nice to see them establish close relationships with each other.

Then there is your medical transition. For every surgery or treatment there will be prep work and recuperation time that needs to be planned, as well as the daunting experience of the procedures themselves. The recovery from each of my four major surgeries was always more challenging than I anticipated, probably due to my optimistic outlook and hopefulness that I would bounce back faster than I actually did. In addition, I had two unanticipated rotator cuff surgeries on my shoulders right in the middle of my transition surgery schedule, which added another layer of complexity, and brought home the lesson that life sometimes gets in the way of your best-laid plans.

Some days I would come home from the office completely drained, but I tried to keep a fitness regimen and work out at the gym every morning, and that routine plus my work took my mind off of any emotional turmoil I was experiencing. What's more, even though I'm completely finished with the transition surgeries, I still have to set aside time every day for aftercare, and this will continue for the foreseeable future.

To prevent all these areas of my life from bleeding into each other, I kept seeing my therapist, Judy, for several months after I transitioned at work. But as the pieces of my post-transition life began fitting together, I didn't need her as much. Judy played a much larger role in helping me figure out what I was going to do before I transitioned, and once I had a plan, I was able to execute it on my own. I still had her support group, and for a while after my first surgeries I continued to go. All of those women were very helpful in showing me how my life would look in the future, and as time went on, they proved to be right. I relied on the older women in the group for guidance but soon I was also giving out advice to newer group members.

This gradual change in my role was consistent with some of the observations shared by other trans women in the group when I asked about how they were maturing into their own transitions after five or ten years. Interestingly, Alice Miller, a long-time member of the group who taught at Stanford University and the Naval War College in Monterey, said she didn't even think about her transition anymore. She told me that after the first few years she settled into her new life and had been happily living it as a woman. The same sentiment was also echoed by Aejaie Sellers, my confidant from Carla's, who mentioned that many of the trans women she works with who start in her group are there for a while as they are coming out, but as they move into their new lives they just live it and don't require as much formal support, and gradually move on.

The eventual completion of your transition and the acceptance of your life in your preferred gender is a very positive outcome, but when you will get there is hard to predict. Obviously, it depends on your family situation and the navigation of other extraneous hurdles, but it will come together for you if you are resolute and have a support system. Slowly but surely, I was able to resolve, or at least come to terms with each of these areas of my life and address them all. Then one day I realized that I had made it. My physical self was aligned with my internal self. I was where I needed to be. As I began to get on with my new life, I didn't really need the support group anymore. I was facing the world as my preferred self, and for the most part, I was happy. And because I had Stella, our family, and a full schedule at work, I was able to drop my other support systems.

Finally, accepting yourself for who you are

I have also come to terms with the realities of my appearance (and really, what woman doesn't share these ongoing disappointments). I eventually realized that genetic women know their own flaws as well as their more positive physical attributes, and trans women do as well. I'm never going to look like Charlize Theron, but I've accepted myself and I'm going to make Dana look the best she can be.

I'm still figuring out ways that I can look more feminine, because I've also come to realize that I will always be a trans person. Since I transitioned later in life and had gone through puberty as a male, the biological consequences have left me with certain physical characteristics that cannot be undone or surgically altered. For example, my height, broader shoulders, and the size of my hands will never change. I will probably never be able to be totally stealth as a woman, even if I wanted to, but I am told that I'm doing a great job of passing, and I am satisfied with that.

I don't know if I will always feel this way about my "transness"—it's too soon to tell. But what I can tell you is that I think it's more important to be comfortable with yourself and who you are, regardless of your appearance. I've met all kinds of women who are constantly unhappy with the way they look, and go for procedure after procedure to "surgically correct" minor flaws, which end up yielding diminishing returns, or worse, create long-term damage. At some point, you have to believe you are your best self. Today, I'm thrilled with my new gender expression to the point that I'm completely out and proud, and I readily advocate for the LGBTQ+ community and transgender people in particular.

When I go to work at my new job, everybody refers to me as Dana, because that's all they know. They all use the right pronouns all the time. At my old job, I would be happy when my co-workers used my correct name or pronouns most of the time, but there was always someone who couldn't ever get it right. But now, I'm the one who slips up and I am secretly thrilled when co-workers correct me! Sometimes I forget myself when I'm in a meeting and think, "Who are they talking about?" until I realize it's me! It's very affirming.

Everything came together at my college reunion

As in all aspects of life, you don't always see your own progress until you have to put it on display for others, or are faced with a life milestone. Both happened to me in 2016 when I was smack in the middle of my medical transition. I saw an email notice that announced the date of my Yale undergraduate class's 40th reunion, which would be held just six months later in June, 2017. The last time I had attended one of these formal reunions, which happen every five years, was my 25th, which was easy to manage because at the time we lived on the East Coast. I remembered it as a great weekend; I saw a lot of friends, and afterwards I stayed in touch with a few of them while we were living in New Jersey, before I moved to California. And, of course, at that time, I was David. So the idea of going to the 40th reunion as Dana was intriguing to say the least. But I wondered, was I really ready to face my past with my new present?

I didn't realize it then, but I began to set the stage almost a year ahead of time, back in the summer of 2016, when I re-emerged as Dana on social media, began writing about my experiences at work in a journal that would eventually become this book, and looking for opportunities to give back to the LGBTQ+ community. At the same time, I was still working and dealing with the less than ideal acceptance of my transition from my company's management.

That fall, after much consideration and discussion with my therapist, I made the decision to have genital surgery, and tried to schedule it as soon as possible. The best my local surgeon in California could offer was a date of the following September, which was nearly a year away. I secured the date but requested to be rescheduled if they could get me in earlier (if there was a cancellation or an unexpected opening).

Then, about three or four months after I changed my Facebook page and my contact information for the college alumni association mailing list to reflect my transition, a good friend from my graduating class tracked me down. Keith was an anesthesiologist in St. Louis, and he sent me a message through the alumni association webmail with a wry comment like, "Boy, things have changed for you." He seemed very positive and happy for me, and we started to communicate by email, saying we should definitely try to get together, perhaps at the next reunion. After that exchange, I decided to at least block my calendar for the reunion dates, and made a hotel reservation just in case I was brave enough to go. I didn't go so far as to officially register for the reunion, but I kept an eye on the growing list of attendees since it was posted on the alumni association's website.

The next important event took place the following March, when I was in New York giving a talk about my career at my medical school alma mater, NYU, and I met with Rachel Bluebond-Langner, a plastic surgeon specializing in transgender procedures who had been recently recruited by NYU to set up a center of excellence for transgender care. I mentioned to her that I was having to wait nearly a year to get my genital surgery in California, and wondered if she would be able to schedule me sooner because we had a personal connection. She told me she would see what she could do and get back to me. Before I left the city, I also met with a literary agent and started discussions about writing this book.

Within a week, Rachel contacted me. She told me that she was able to move another appointment around and offered to squeeze me in early May. I accepted it in a heartbeat. I was so excited that I would finally be taking the last step toward womanhood!

At home, I started to make preparations for taking what would be my last medical leave from work. I knew I would be gone for a few weeks and had to figure out all of the logistics of my travel and accommodations in New York for the recuperation. The support staff at NYU connected me with a great apartment building which had a special arrangement with the university for housing post-operative patients, so I booked an extended stay. That's when I realized that attending the reunion was becoming more of a possibility.

I carefully considered how I wanted to approach the event. What kind of reception was I going to get? It would definitely be strange just walking in as my new self—what would these people who only thought of me as David for 40 years think now? I knew Keith, the anesthesiologist, was going to be supportive, but really hadn't had contact with anyone else. Then I remembered the alumni magazine came out monthly and included class updates in every issue, where classmates would share what was going on in their lives. I decided to contact the class secretary and send in an "update" about me, which I had never done before. My hope was to have it appear in an issue before the reunion. This way, anyone who read it wouldn't be taken completely by surprise.

My graduating class was around 1200 people, so I didn't know all of them, but I did recognize the class secretary's name. We had rowed on the crew team together during my freshman year. I remembered him as a nice guy but didn't know whether he was conservative or liberal, so I wasn't sure how a communication of this nature would be received. I don't recall ever seeing anything about transgender transitions in any prior issues. It turned out that he was incredibly supportive and generous, and he pulled a few strings to get my update into the issue of the magazine which came out right before the reunion. This is what was printed:

> I heard from our classmate, *Dave Pizzuti*, who is now known as *Dana Pizzuti* after her gender transition. Dana has been working [in the pharmaceutical industry] in California since 2007. "I completed medical school at NYU, did five years of specialty and subspecialty training, and have spent 30 years as an executive in the pharmaceutical industry. Since my transition in 2015, I began advocacy work for the transgender community to support the process of transitions, especially in the workplace, and to ensure access to healthcare in the current turbulent environment. I'm collaborating with the UCSF Center of Excellence in Transgender Health in San Francisco, the NYU Langone Center for Transgender Health in New York City, and the Howard Brown Clinic in Chicago, in addition to continuing my work [in the pharmaceutical industry]. I'm also writing a book to provide guidelines and strategies for transgender individuals, their co-workers, and Human Resources professionals to achieve successful gender transitions in the workplace. My wife and I are planning to attend the reunion in June, and I am looking forward to reconnecting with classmates."

As May approached, I was making the final preparations for my surgery and travel. Ever the optimist, I planned for only three weeks of recuperation after the surgery, which was on the short end of the medical post-op recommendations. I should have been more realistic and planned for a longer recovery; this was just another example of letting my hopes overrule my common sense. The plan was to fly home around May 24 and then, if I was up to it physically and still wanted to go to the reunion, I would fly back East a week later on June 1. Not knowing what would be happening at work or whether I could feasibly travel such a long distance so soon, I still had not officially registered for the reunion, but I didn't cancel my New Haven hotel, either.

May couldn't come soon enough. When the day finally arrived, I flew out to New York for the pre-operative doctor's visits and to get ready for surgery. The procedure went very well and I was so thrilled to finally have my body be congruent with my mind, but the recuperation was a bit more challenging than I had expected. Thankfully, Stella had accompanied me to New York and was wonderful during the first two weeks of the recovery. Once she saw that I was settled into a pretty good routine, she decided to go back home for a few days to see her kids.

I tried to stay as active as possible, and since the weather was beautiful, every day I walked around Manhattan for hours; sitting was uncomfortable. I was hoping to go home to California and then return to attend the reunion in June. Then I had a bit of a medical setback: the surgeon didn't think I was ready to fly back to California for another ten days.

I had a decision to make: should I fly home as quickly as I could and get back to work, skipping the reunion, or stay in New York just a couple of days longer and go directly to New Haven? I was conflicted about a number of issues: first, I would be missing more days of work even though I had been very active on emails and attending conference calls from New York during my recovery. I was struggling with my new boss, and continued to deal with the company's attitude toward my "level of engagement." Second, by this time I had already attended the Out & Equal Conference, which was when I decided to start to look for a more supportive work opportunity. While I was in New York, I was being recruited for positions at other employers, including the one at Rigel. There was a possibility that I needed to be in California for potential interviews. However, my literary agent was shopping around with the proposal for this book, and I might have to meet with publishers in New York.

In the end, I decided it was really important for me to attend the reunion because I was ready for my past to meet my present. The 40th reunion was going to be a big deal, and if I missed it there wouldn't be another one for five years, and who knows where I would be then. I also learned that some of my classmates who were registered to attend were authors or journalists, and would be holding writing and publishing seminars. Several had long careers working with *The Wall Street Journal*, *The Washington Post* and *The New Yorker*, which would be important connections to have once my book was published. Meeting up with them would be an added benefit since I could learn something about the publishing world from knowledgeable accomplished writers. On the very last day of the open registration, I put my name down on the list and rented a car to drive to New Haven. Unfortunately, Stella was not able to join me as she had to stay in California with her kids.

The only problem was that I hadn't brought the right clothes for this type of event. The outfits I had planned to wear were back in California. I had to go shopping and buy some formal shoes and less casual tops. So I went to Barneys and made new friends with a few salespeople at the two stores in Manhattan. I bought a few things from the hipper Chelsea store, and a few things from the more upscale Madison Avenue shop. I have to say, I looked good, and was satisfied that I was ready to face my classmates.

On May 31, I got to New Haven after several uncomfortable hours in traffic, but when I arrived it was a gorgeous day, and the weather stayed that way the entire weekend. The whole event was going to be incredible. Once I checked into the hotel, I decided to take a stroll around the campus and reconnect with the town. The seminars started the next day and the actual reunion was going to be the day after, so that first day I was on my own. Just the sights and sounds of my old college town, walking around on a beautiful day as a woman, was so encouraging and satisfying. I thought back to my days at school and how I knew that something was different about me, but I was unaware of my options or where those feelings would eventually lead.

The next day I went into the main building where we were supposed to register, which was actually the residential hall where I spent two years of my college life, right in the center of campus. There was the registration table, where everyone grabbed their name tag, and I saw mine that read: *Dana Pizzuti, MD*. When I looked around I realized there were a lot of people I didn't really know at all, and some who had only been acquaintances. Then I saw Keith, who had tracked me down last fall. He came over and gave me a big hug, and we were inseparable for the rest of the time. I hung out with him and a group of his friends, a few of whom I had stayed in touch with over the years, as well as their wives. One of the wives, whom I had known when she was dating another of my friends during college, said to me, "You look so fantastic; I was telling Sue that you're such a bitch looking better than we do.' And I laughed and said, "That's the most affirming thing I've ever heard! I know I have finally arrived!"

During one of the dinners that weekend I remember going to get a drink and some food when another classmate came over and told me that she had read my story in the alumni magazine: I was so pleased that at least somebody had read my update. At another point, the chair of the alumni association, who was in my class, came over and sat down with me and said, "What you're doing is so important." I thanked her and told her I was so excited to be there and I wanted to know if there was anything I could do to help advocate for LGBTQ+ students or alumni. She eventually connected me with someone on the alumni association and we have since stayed in touch. I also made a point to go to the class secretary and thank him for being so sensitive about putting my announcement into the class notes in time to be published before the event.

All in all, I hadn't felt such open-hearted acceptance since I came out to my work teams two years earlier. The weekend exceeded all of my expectations. I reconnected with a lot of people, and made new friends. As a result of the contact within the alumni association, I was invited to come back and sit on an LGBTQ+ career panel in New Haven the following April for students and young alumni. I was also asked to participate in a discussion panel on transgender issues in San Francisco in March. It would have been so easy to let my old life go; I probably never would have connected again with any of those people. But because I put myself out there, that one weekend opened up a whole new network for me that was always there but I was not accessing. It really shows that anyone from your prior life, even if they never had any contact at all with trans people, can really be supportive and happy for you. I learned that weekend that you should never be afraid to revisit your past or move bravely forward into the future.

It's your turn

By now, you've learned a thing or two from this book that will make your workplace transition go smoothly so that you can confidently become the person you want to be. I hope this book can help and encourage you to be your true self and be ready for anything that comes your way. As you've read, the only guarantee is that there will be many challenges and setbacks along your path. Being prepared for as many contingencies as possible will help minimize the obstacles and smooth your journey to your preferred gender.

As my friend Pips Bunce told me, "You may encounter very anti-trans or bigoted people, but for every one bigoted person, you're going to come across thousands of others who are loving, accepting, compassionate, inclusive, and open-minded. At work, there will be many different kinds of reactions to the various trans identities or to someone's transition. Don't be put off by your fears of negativity because you'll be amazed at all the loving and caring people who are waiting to support you, especially when you first make your declaration. I was amazed at how many people had my back, and clearly expressed how I inspired them by having the courage to embrace my true self. Most people really admire someone having the confidence to be truly authentic in who they are, and I was genuinely touched by what amazing allies they have been."

This book represents my experience, but there's no one best route or plan for everyone. Your internal and external worlds are constantly evolving and will be different from anyone else's. The most important thing is to devise ways to integrate and adjust your plans based on changes to your personal situation as well as changes to the world going on around you. Trans people will always face obstacles and these are challenging times. I hope that every one of us can help our cause by being the best we can be, which means being even a little better than everyone else in how we do our job and how we treat each other. We're all advocates and allies, and we can collectively prove to the world that it's essential that we live our lives authentically.

GLOSSARY

Affordable Care Act: Patient Protection and Affordable Care Act: often shortened to the **Affordable Care Act** (**ACA**) or nicknamed **Obamacare**, this was signed into law by President Barack Obama in 2010. The ACA increases health insurance coverage to all Americans. This legislation is important because it provides an additional source of coverage for transgender healthcare.

Ally: Allies can be an individual or group of individuals that are associated with one another to support a common cause or purpose. An ally in the context of transgender inclusion policies in the workplace refers to those people who choose to support their transgender colleagues.

American Civil Liberties Union (ACLU): a non-partisan, non-profit organization whose stated mission is "to defend and preserve the individual rights and liberties guaranteed to every person in this country by the Constitution and laws of the United States." Local affiliates of the ACLU are active in almost all 50 states, the District of Columbia, and Puerto Rico. The ACLU frequently represents transgender individuals in cases of harassment and discrimination.

Bottom surgery: a colloquial term for genital alterations in transgender surgery. It refers to gender-affirming genital surgeries, including vaginoplasty or zero depth vulvectomy for MTF trans people, or phalloplasty and metoidioplasty for FTM trans people.

Breast augmentation: a medical procedure for transitioning MTF trans people, which entails the insertion of prostheses under the chest muscles to create breasts.

Chondrolaryngoplasty: more commonly called **tracheal shave**, this is a surgical facial feminization procedure in which the thyroid cartilage is reduced in size by shaving down the cartilage (the Adam's apple).

Cisgender/cis: anyone who identifies as the sex they were assigned at birth.

Closeted: when an LGBTQ+ person hides their true sexual orientation or preferred gender expression from the public, including those closest to them. People stay closeted often out of fear, but others choose to be closeted because they see no reason to make their gender preferences or identity public.

Cross-dressing: the act of wearing items of clothing and accessories commonly associated with the opposite sex. A **cross-dresser** is often synonymous with the term **transvestite**. Both of these terms typically refer to the clothes a person is wearing, and does not infer a decision made as to a person's sexuality or preferred gender expression.

Diagnostic and Statistical Manual of Mental Disorders: published by the American Psychiatric Association, a reference book that offers a common language and standard criteria for the classification of mental disorders. It is used, or relied on, by clinicians, researchers, health insurance companies, pharmaceutical companies, the legal system, and policy makers among others. The most current DSM (DSM-5) does not list either homosexuality or gender dysphoria as psychiatric disorders.

Electrolysis: a method of permanently removing individual hairs from the face or body. The process destroys the growth center of the hair with chemical or heat energy. After a very fine probe is inserted into the hair follicle, the hair is removed with tweezers. Most areas of the body can be treated with electrolysis, including the eyebrows, face, abdomen, thighs, breasts, pubic region, and legs.

Employee resource group (ERG): a group of employees who join together in a workplace based on shared characteristics or life experiences. Also known as affinity group or business network group.

Endocrinologist: a physician who specializes in the endocrine system, its diseases, and its specific secretions known as hormones. An endocrinologist is the most knowledgeable resource for prescribing hormone therapies.

Facial feminization surgery: a set of surgical procedures that alter male facial features to bring them closer in shape and size to typical female facial features. FFS can include a brow lift, rhinoplasty (change to the structure of the nose), cheek implantation, Adam's apple reduction, and lip augmentation.

FTM: female to male, acronym used to describe people who were assigned female at birth but live and identify as men, and sometimes transition medically.

Gender dysphoria: the distress a person experiences as a result of the gender they were assigned at birth, when the biological gender does not match the person's gender identity. Also known as gender identity disorder (GID).

Gender expression: the external appearance of a person's preferred gender identity, which could encompass behavior, clothing, haircut, or voice quality, and which may or may not conform to defined masculine or feminine behaviors and characteristics.

Gender fluid: a description of someone who does not identify themselves as having a fixed gender. A person who is gender fluid may feel male some days, and female other days. Being gender fluid has nothing to do with which set of genitalia one has, nor one's sexual orientation. Gender fluid individuals use pronouns based on how they feel in the moment.

Gender identity: the inherent feeling within an individual of what gender they are. It can encompass not only male and female, but anything in between or outside the gender spectrum.

Gender neutral: a classification for individuals who do not feel that they belong to either gender. Gender neutral individuals use they/them pronouns.

Gender non-conforming: a description denoting a person whose behavior or appearance does not conform to prevailing cultural and social expectations about what is appropriate for their gender. Gender non-conforming individuals use they/them or ze/zim/zir pronouns.

Gender/genital reassignment surgery (GRS): the surgical procedure (or procedures) by which a transgender person's genital appearance and function are altered to resemble and function as their preferred gender. It is part of a treatment for gender dysphoria.

Hormone replacement therapy (HRT): when referring to transgender hormone therapy, it is a form of hormone replacement therapy in which sex hormones and other hormonal medications are administered to transgender individuals for the purpose of more closely aligning their secondary sexual characteristics with their gender identity. This form of HRT is given as one of two types, based on whether the goal of treatment is feminization or masculinization. HRT should always be administered under a doctor's care.

Inclusion and diversity group: a distinct subgroup, usually within the HR department, whose purpose is to champion and educate employees and managers on how to sensitively operate within a diverse and open workplace environment.

Internist: a physician who specializes in the diagnosis and medical treatment of adults. An internist can also prescribe HRT.

Laser hair removal: the process of hair removal by pulsing laser light that destroys a hair follicle. It became commercially available in the mid-1990s. Laser works best with dark coarse hair. Light skin and dark hair are an ideal combination. White hair, light blond and strawberry blond hair does not respond well to this treatment.

LGBTQ+: refers to lesbian, gay, bisexual, trans, queer/questioning, and intersex individuals.

Licensed clinical social worker (LCSW): a trained social worker who holds a master's degree in social work, and has three years of supervised experience and continuing education. LCSWs are able to perform a variety of functionally similar mental health therapies and diagnostic procedures. These therapists cannot prescribe medications, but often run support groups as well as provide individual counseling.

Mastectomy: also referred to as **chest masculinization** or **top surgery** for FTM, is the removal of unwanted breast tissue in order to create a masculine chest appearance.

Medicaid: a joint federal and state insurance program for individuals of all ages whose income and resources are insufficient to pay for healthcare. The ACA, or Obamacare, significantly expanded both eligibility for and federal funding of Medicaid. Medicaid is the nation's largest insurer, funding a significant portion of national spending on personal healthcare and providing low- or no-cost health coverage to nearly 70 million people—including many LGBTQ+ individuals. LGBTQ+ people are more likely than non-LGBTQ+ people to be living in poverty and to be uninsured. Overall, one in five Americans receives health insurance coverage through Medicaid in any given year.

Medicare: the federal health insurance program for people who are 65 or older, certain younger people with disabilities, and people with end-stage renal disease. There is currently no national exclusion for transition-related healthcare under Medicare. This means that coverage decisions for transition-related surgeries will be made individually on the basis of medical need and applicable standards of care, similar to other medical services provided under Medicare. Medicare also covers medically necessary hormone therapy for transgender people. These medications are part of the Medicare Part D prescription drug plan.

Metoidioplasty or metaoidioplasty: FTM gender/genital-reassignment surgery in which testosterone replacement therapy gradually enlarges the clitoris. A surgeon then separates the enlarged clitoris from the labia in order to lower it to the approximate position of a penis.

Mis-gender: referring to or addressing someone using pronouns that do not correctly reflect the gender with which they identify or express.

MTF: male to female, acronym used to describe people who were assigned male at birth but live and identify as women, and sometimes transition medically.

National Center for Transgender Equality (NCTE): a non-profit, social equality organization in the US founded in 2003 by transgender activist Mara Keisling. The organization aims to advance the equality of transgender people. NCTE focuses on discrimination in employment, access to public accommodations, fair housing, identity documents, hate crimes and violence, criminal justice reform, federal research surveys, and healthcare access, among other important issues for trans people.

Non-binary: a description of people born with bodies that may fit typical definitions of male and female, but their innate gender identity is something other than male or female. Non-binary individuals use they/them pronouns.

Orchiectomy: a gender-affirming genital surgical procedure that removes the testicles for MTF trans people.

Out & Equal Workplace Advocates: an LGBTQ+ workplace advocacy non-profit organization with headquarters in San Francisco, California. Its vision is to achieve workplace equality for all regardless of sexual orientation, gender identity, expression, or characteristics. Out & Equal provides training and resources to LGBTQ+ employees and corporations.

OUTstanding: a membership organization for global businesses that works directly with LGBTQ+ and ally leaders to drive cultural change. Based in the UK, this organization is an association supported by some of the largest corporations, creating a network that can be leveraged to drive positive change.

Passing: a transgender person's ability to be correctly perceived as the gender they identify as and not be perceived as transgender.

Passing privilege: a term for the benefits that come with being taken for cis by cis people.

Phalloplasty: a set of gender-affirming genital surgical procedures that creates a penis for FTM trans people.

Psychiatrist: a physician that specializes in treating a patient's well-being, focusing primarily on disorders such as a chemical imbalance. Psychiatrists can prescribe medications for depression and anxiety, among others.

Psychologist: a licensed mental health professional with an advanced degree who is not able to write prescriptions but may recommended a patient be seen by a psychiatrist in order to receive medications. Their primary focus is on a patient's thoughts, feelings and general mental health, and treatment can include individual counseling and support groups.

Sexual orientation: who an individual is sexually and/or emotionally attracted to. Trans people can identify as straight, gay, lesbian, bisexual, asexual, pansexual, and so on. Sexual orientation describes who you date; gender identity describes who you are.

Sexual reassignment surgery (SRS): surgical procedures to obtain physical characteristics found in the opposite gender. SRS may encompass bottom surgery or top surgery. In some states, SRS is required to change one's legal gender.

Stealth: when a transgender person passes so well that no one is aware of their transgender history. Some transgender people who live stealth feel no need to disclose their history; others do not disclose for safety or employment reasons. It is sometimes used in the phrase "living stealth."

Title VII: a federal law, part of the Civil Rights Act of 1964, that prohibits employers from discriminating against employees on the basis of sex (gender), race, color, national origin, and religion. It generally applies to employers with 15 or more employees, including federal, state, and local governments. Title VII also applies to private and public colleges and universities, employment agencies, and labor organizations. Despite Title VII's passage, transgender discrimination in the workplace remains a serious problem.

Top surgery: a colloquial term for alterations in transgender surgery that affect the chest and breasts. It refers to gender-affirming surgeries including breast augmentation for MTF trans people, or mastectomy for FTM trans people.

Transgender: an individual who does not identify with the sex they were assigned at birth. Transgender or **trans** is the umbrella term that encompasses multiple gender-related identities.

Transgender Law Center (TLC): the largest transgender-focused civil rights organization in the US. The stated mission of the TLC is to connect transgender people and their families to technically sound and culturally competent legal services, to increase acceptance and enforcement of laws and policies, and to work to change laws and systems that fail to incorporate the needs and experiences of transgender people.

Transitioning: the process of transitioning socially, emotionally, and/or physically from one gender to another. Some regard transitioning as a period of time from a few months/years to many years; others feel that there is a definite period of transitioning with a point of completion, and others feel that it is a long-term, ever-evolving process. Some transgender people, post-transition, no longer consider themselves as transgender. Others feel that they are in a state of transition for the rest of their lives.

Transvestite: a person, typically a man, who derives pleasure from dressing in clothes primarily associated with women. Transvestite should not be confused with transgender; transvestites are often happy with their gender and have no desire to change, but simply enjoy being able to cross-dress from time to time.

Vaginoplasty: a gender-affirming genital surgical procedure that creates a vagina for MTF trans people.

World Professional Association for Transgender Health (WPATH): a professional organization devoted to the understanding and treatment of gender dysphoria. WPATH is most known for publishing the *Standards of Care for the Health of Transsexual, Transgender, and Gender Nonconforming People*, but also provides information for professionals and consumers, sponsors scientific conferences, and offers ethical guidelines for health insurance coverage. The first version of the *Standards of Care* was published in 1979. The latest edition, Version 7, was published in 2011.

INDEX